The Welfare of America 2:

A Guide for Supporting Effective Policies that Promote the Prosperity and Stability of the United States

By

Rodney W. Black

INTRODUCTION

My most significant life experience begins at age eight as a struggling Little League Baseball player who failed to catch a single fly ball in the right field and get a single hit during my dismal first season. Though I would eventually improve and experience brief periods of glory on the baseball diamond, I would finally learn that I would never become a Major League baseball player. Nonetheless, my experience as a Little Leaguer taught me to work hard and make the most out of my talents.

After graduating from high school, I joined the United States Air Force Security Police (now Security Forces), serving at Travis Air Force Base in Northern California. My time as a security policeman taught me how to endure minor hardships and the importance of serving my nation.

This is my police academy graduating class at Los Medanos College in Pittsburg, California. I am in the bottom row, third from left.

After being honorably discharged from the Air Force, I decided to continue pursuing a law enforcement career. In the spring of 1990, I entered the Los Medanos College Police Academy as a non-sponsored cadet, meaning any police department did not yet hire me. I had to pay my way through the academy. After a few failed attempts at securing a job as a police officer, I decided to complete my bachelor's degree in Criminal Justice at Sacramento State University. Though I never worked for a police department, my experience as a police academy graduate taught me police work difficulties.

Then in 1997, I embarked on my most significant experience yet. I joined the Peace Corps as a community health education extensionist. As a Peace Corps volunteer on Wakenaam Island, Guyana, I educated community members about health and organized a handful of community development projects. Eventually, I helped create Wakenaam Island's first library/computer lab. I introduced computers to Wakenaam Island residents. Most significantly, I met my current wife, Mohanie Ramsahai, during the summer of 1997. We got married in December 1999.

In this picture, I am briefing Guyana President Janet Jagan on the Wakenaam Learning Center Project. This picture was taken at the United States Embassy in Georgetown, Guyana.

As a former socialist country, Guyana struggled to free itself from the shackles of dependence on foreign aid and the International Development Bank/World Bank loans. My time in Guyana reinforced my belief that socialism is a failed economic system that leads nations into poverty. My experience as a Peace Corps volunteer also taught me that the capacity-building approach is the best way to provide economic opportunity to underserved populations and communities. Moreover, I witnessed how immigration detrimentally impacts developing countries. Since Guyana is one of the poorest countries in the western hemisphere, many Guyanese citizens aspire to immigrate to England, Canada, and the United States to pursue more significant opportunities.

Since the migration arrows are pointing away from Guyana and western capitalist countries, Guyana lost many of its talented citizens over the years, the type of citizens a nation needs to thrive and prosper. Furthermore, since a substantial number of Guyanese people have relatives living abroad, many Guyanese people saw their living situation in Guyana as temporary, causing them to take less ownership of the nation's problems. This lack of ownership weakened the social contract within between Guyanese people. Fortunately, Guyana discovered oil off its shores and has a new president, creating more significant potential opportunities for Guyanese people and reversing the migration arrows.

After completing my two-year service in the Peace Corps, I obtained a job as a financial planner at Prudential Financial Planning

Services, a Prudential Insurance Company division. Although I learned a lot about finances during my brief stay at Prudential, I realized that being a financial planner was not my true calling. Thanks to an encounter with one of my old gym buddies, I would find my true calling: teaching. My friend advised me to obtain my two-year preliminary teaching credential in California through my Peace Corps teaching experience. And as luck would have it, I found a job teaching Health/Health Science CTE in Sacramento, California, in 2000.

The past twenty years have been interesting. The United States survived its first contested election in Bush VS. Gore in 2000. The United States briefly united after Al-Qaeda destroyed the World Trade Center Towers and damaged the Pentagon. After completing a tumultuous eight years in the White House, President Bush handed the reigns to Senator Obama, making the junior senator from Illinois the first African American president in the nation's history, a moment of pride for the country.

It is easy to dislike President Trump's personality; he presents himself as arrogant, bombastic, crude, and self-interested. President Trump has made many inarticulate statements in rallies and on Twitter throughout the past five years, arousing his angry opponents' passions. This country has arguably not been this divided since the Civil War. Partisans amplify their rhetoric, contributing to the divisiveness and hate that are sweeping across this nation. Though angry partisan Americans are not killing each other in the streets yet, our politicians and the powerful elites who put them in power need to reflect on our current state of chaos. There is a reason for hope, however.

Since the pandemic began in March, I used my free time to engage in a deep intellectual dive to enhance my knowledge and make sense of the world. I discovered and rediscovered some great thinkers on the Intellectual Dark Web (IDW) during this time. A term coined by Dr. Eric Weinstein, managing director of Thiel Capital and the older brother of Professor Brett Weinstein, the Intellectual Dark Web consists of intellectuals who defend free speech, oppose cancel culture and political correctness, and oppose partisan politics. Their views are primarily heterodox, meaning their opinions transcend partisan political politics. Members of the Intellectual Dark Web—consisting of Brett Weinstein, Eric Weinstein, Heather Heying, Coleman Hughes, Jonathan Haidt, Maajid Nawaz, Debra Soh, Sam Harris, Joe Rogan, Dave Rubin, Glenn Loury, John Mcwhorter, Jordan Peterson, and others —spread their heterodox messages through YouTube and other platforms.

My emersion into the Intellectual Dark Web world has provided me hope for the nation's future. By viewing these contemporary thought-leaders from the IDW, I realize that there are men and women of goodwill in this country—patriotic men and women confronting our nation's destructive forces. They are not the stooges of the Democratic Party or the Republican Party; they are independent thinkers. These thought-leaders apply their sound judgment and analysis to politics and current events, conspicuously absent from most of our mainstream media.

As a nation, we need to allow the IDW to take the lead in our political debate. We need to demand that our political leaders and their influential supporters have their ideas challenged in thoughtful, thorough, and respectful discussions. The leaders of the IDW can facilitate this process.

CHAPTER 1: THE SIX FILTERS OF SITUATIONAL ANALYSIS

To make sense of the world, one needs to have critical thinking skills, which people lack. The process that everyone follows when making decisions varies from person to person. Many of us employ a simple process that can lead to faulty analysis and decision-making, while some employ a complex process that can lead to quality analysis and decision-making. The evidence of faulty analysis is ubiquitous. For example, when the media covers police shootings, they often exclude essential details because of inadequate analysis. The media fails to thoroughly analyze the role of the suspect/victim's behavior in the officer's actions. They also fail to report these stories properly by providing an accurate statistical analysis of the frequency of these deadly encounters, making it seem that these encounters occur more frequently (availability heuristics). This bias analysis is emblematic of the divergent thinking that divides our nation along political lines.

Divergent thinking among the masses reminds us of the fragility of democracies. Why do people support certain politicians (Joe Biden or Donald Trump) and specific political causes (Black Lives Matter or the Tea Party)? How is it possible for two people representing the same demographics groups to arrive at radically different opinions when interpreting an idea or event (whether to support the COVID lockdown, raise taxes on the rich, or defund the police)? Divergent thinking occurs because people analyze ideas or events through different filters, or in most cases, not enough filters. Nevertheless, there are several possible filters one might use to interpret an idea or analyze a situation. Critical thinkers can analyze ideas, situations, and current events through these six cognitive filters:

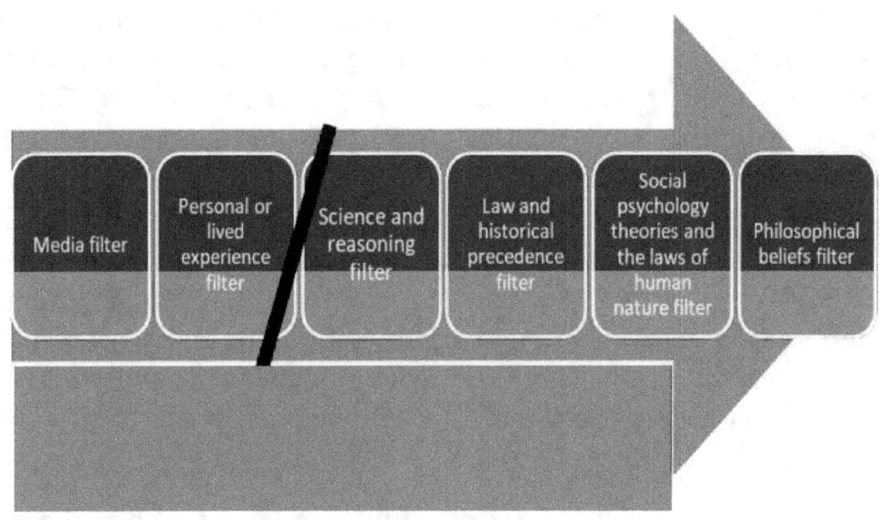

Most of us consciously and unconsciously analyze ideas or events through various filters before forming opinions or making decisions. For example, an analytical thinker might investigate, analyze, and interpret a weaker-than-expected job report through several filters before arriving at a well-informed conclusion. This methodical approach of analyzing ideas and events through several cognitive filters arguably produces the best results.

The news media filter:

Since most of us receive our information from the media, many of us might rely on the media to provide accurate, non-biased information, causing us to form our ideas or opinions of a particular event based on the news report itself. During the social media age, the media have become more biased in their reporting. News outlets—such as the New York Times, Washington Post, Washington Times, CNN, MSNBC, and Fox News feed their social media echo chambers what they want to see and hear, making the news more biased and less reliable than the era when independent media and the big-three news networks dominated journalism. Since the news media are less reliable than before, we should view most news stories with skepticism. It is not uncommon for news outlets to retract news stories. For instance, several news outlets retracted a story that initially claimed that Capitol protestors beat Officer Brian Sicknick with a fire extinguisher. The New York Times and the Washington Post recently retracted a story relating the FBI raid on former New York Mayor Rudy Giuliani's apartment. There are too many examples to delineate in this book, but recent polling relating to trust in the media tells us not to trust everything we see or hear in the media. The media serve a useful purpose, however.

When we watch or read a story from the media, we should consider that story a starting point in the analytical process. News stories alert us when actual events occur; they provide the public with specific facts. For instance, when George Floyd died in Derick Chauvin's hands last summer, the media provided important specific facts that lawyers proved in court during Derick Chauvin's trial. The initial reporting from television and print media indicated that George Floyd was under the influence of drugs, attempted to pass a counterfeit twenty-dollar bill, and resisted arrest. The initial reports also indicated that officer Derick Chauvin had his knee on George Floyd's neck for over nine minutes. Though lawyers proved these facts correct in court, analytical thinkers typically resist forming opinions without analyzing the facts through the six filters. The life or lived experience filter is another essential filter that everyone uses to analyze ideas and events.

The personal or lived experience filter:

The analytical thinker might filter the job report through life experience, conjuring up fears of living through stagflation (high inflation, high unemployment, and stagnant economic growth) again. Anyone who lived through the 1970s remembers long gas lines and high interest rates. However, an analytical thinker understands the dangers of analyzing an idea or event through the personal or lived experience filter alone. Since everyone cannot experience everything in life, analyzing a job report through the personal or lived experience filter alone can result in faulty analysis; thus, the analytical thinker will analyze the job report through additional filters.

It is not necessarily fallacious to judge ideas and events through the life experiences lens. Many scientific discoveries begin with personal observations, which form hypotheses. Scientists often test their hypotheses by employing the scientific method (another filer). Additionally, people with varied and significant life experiences often advance to the top of our competence hierarchies.   Ideally, we want people who have traveled worldwide and experienced various political and economic systems to serve our government. We want our politicians to be worldly, wise, and well-cultured. We also want our politicians to have military experience, business experience, public service experience, and significant leadership experience. General Colin Powell epitomizes this experience. General Powell climbed Army ranks to become Chairman of the Joint Chiefs of Staff and eventually became the first African American secretary of state. Americans clamored for General Powell to run for president, but he declined.

Americans are reluctant to send their young men and women to fight a war without a well-articulated national security interest. Americans seem to be even more reluctant to send their sons and daughters to war when the commander-in-chief has never served in the military. For this reason, it is helpful when our president has the first-hand experience in the military to understand the horrors of war, making General Powell a viable presidential candidate in voters' eyes. One must wonder if Vice President Dick Cheney, who never served in the military, would have supported attacking Iraq if he had served in the Vietnam War.

Our politicians make decisions regarding taxes, trade, and business regulations that often produce unintended consequences. Voters can mitigate these unintended consequences by voting for candidates who have business experience. Politicians who have the lived experience of making payroll and navigating confusing regulations are more likely to empathize with small business owners before voting for new taxes and regulations. One must wonder how Bernie Sanders, Alexandria Ocasio-Cortez, and other Democratic Socialists' views might change if they had to operate a hot dog cart in Manhattan for a year.

Though we learn the best lessons in life through personal experience, personal experience is often unreliable and too insignificant to trust when analyzing ideas and events. We know through research that eyewitness testimony is often unreliable in court. The popular television news program 60 Minutes produced a critical story about a rape survivor who falsely selected Ronald Cotton in a police photo line. The 60 Minutes story teaches us that memory is fallible and open to suggestions. Critical thinkers also know that our limited life experiences, inability to live another person's shoes, biases, prejudices, and political ideology alter our perceptions about specific ideas and how we judge events, such as George Floyd's death. For example, one might commit the fundamental attribution error by blaming dispositional factors for a waitress's poor service instead of considering situational factors—such as the restaurant not having enough staff or being busy.

Everyone is guilty of committing the fundamental attribution error. We commit this fatal error when we cuss out a driver for cutting us off on the freeway. Thus, we automatically assume that the driver is careless, reckless, and stupid. We do not consider possible situational factors that might explain the erratic driving. Moreover, we are more likely to commit the fundamental attribution error if stigma consciousness is part of the equation. Stigma consciousness can result when we expect to be treated a certain way because of our membership in certain underrepresented or marginalized groups. A 5' 4" high school student might accuse his coach of heightism of being cut from the basketball team, causing him to ignore the possible situational factors.

When we rely on personal or lived experience, we often use heuristics and mental shortcuts that save time but lead to errors when making sense of specific situations. Police officers use heuristics when assessing situations to avoid the laborious, time-consuming process of analyzing a situation before taking action in deadly situations. We also use heuristical thinking when assessing how often certain problematic occurrences occur based on frequent media coverage. For instance, since shark attacks are infrequent, the media extensively covers them, making shark attacks seem more problematic than they are. We can make the same argument about Islamic terrorist attacks in the United States. Since these terror attacks happen so infrequently, the media cover them extensively, making us think they are more problematic than they are.

The science and reasoning filter:

The fallibility of lived experience requires reasonable people to analyze information through additional filters. Arguably, the science and reasoning filter is the most reliable of the six filters as long as the science is not rooted in fraud and corrupted by political ideology. The enlightenment thinkers modernized science and revolutionized the scientific method. Scientists employ the scientific method by relying on skepticism to overcome erroneous assumptions that lived experience or personal observations might produce. Every accepted scientific fact that we take for granted has faced intense scrutiny throughout the years. For instance, NASA can accurately deliver probes to any planets in our solar system. Science and math converge, making it is possible to deliver a rover to Mars.

The science of vaccines has evolved significantly since Edward Jenner inoculated James Phipps, an eight-year-old boy, with the cowpox virus, which ultimately protected him from smallpox. Since Jenner's experiment, other scientists have employed the scientific method to create vaccines to fight other diseases, such as measles, mumps, rubella, polio, influenza, and COVID 19. After the COVID 19 vaccine survived clinical trials, millions of people worldwide trusted science and the scientific method to save their lives. Many of us will base our decision on whether to receive the COVID vaccine on science and the scientific method.

When it comes to political arguments, many of us use logic to analyze the merit of a particular claim. Our reliance on inaccurate, biased information in the media often induces us to commit the fallacy of the hasty generalization, concluding without having all the facts. Activists often commit this fallacy when they conclude police shooting without having all the facts. Media personalities and politicians are often guilty of the ad hominem fallacy, a common practice in the Trump era. Purveyors of woke ideology often commit the false dichotomy fallacy when they argue that one can only be racist or antiracist (as the woke activists define). Critical thinkers understand that most people do not think in black and white terms, that they mostly fall in the middle.

Nevertheless, emotions drive extreme thinking, and extreme thinking causes people to see the world in black and white terms. The appeal to emotion and bandwagon appeal is driving extreme elements of both political parties. With our emotions high and pervasive need to feel accepted, many of our fellow Americans are joining movements rooted in lousy ideology, such as defunding the police campaign.

Social critics and activists often rely on hidden assumptions in their arguments. For instance, an activist might imply that discrimination causes a specific disparity between groups without providing evidence of the existence of discrimination. Coleman Hughes, the remarkable young intellectual, calls this racism of the gaps. Those who embed hidden assumptions in their arguments also commit the fallacy of oversimplification, the error of identifying a single cause of the problem as the actual problem while ignoring other potential causes. After all, no reasonable person would argue that discrimination and racism do not exist. A reasonable person would acknowledge other potential causes of a particular problem before concluding.

A famous conservative radio talk show host says, "Hell is a place where there is no reason." Critical thinking and reasoning work symbiotically to analyze the merits of an argument and evaluate a specific event's circumstances. Our failure to think critically will only cause us to subscribe to a faulty ideology, adopt bad ideas, or succumb to emotional reasoning, which, according to Professor Jonathan Haidt, occurs when we allow our emotions to guide our interpretation of reality.

Establishing correlations between variables and ultimately cause/effect relationships is essential for analyzing problems and events. When leftists embed hidden assumptions in their claims, they also employ another intellectual misdirection by employing the voiding of the causes strategY. When these intellectually dishonest actors employ the voiding of the inconvenient causes strategy, they fail to consider all potential causes of a problem. Instead, they fixate on a potential cause supporting their political narrative, discounting causes that disprove their political narrative. For example, President Biden signed an executive order closing the Keystone Pipeline project. When gas prices increased, President Biden and his supporters voided the Keystone Pipeline decision as a possible cause of an increase in gas prices. De-policing and de-incarceration advocates are voiding the inconvenient causes by failing to acknowledge that eliminating cash bail for criminal defendants, defunding the police, failing to charge certain criminal defendants, and releasing inmates from jail or prison because of

COVID concerns are significant causes of a violent crime spike in major cities throughout the United States.

According to the Centers for Disease Control, obesity correlates with adverse COVID outcomes. However, this apparent link between obesity and COVID makes our politicians and public health experts downplay the relationship between obesity and hospitalizations/deaths because of political convenience. This lack of an apparent causal link between COVID and adverse health outcomes diminishes the personal responsibility argument, stating that our destructive health behaviors correlate with adverse health outcomes. Instead, politicians and public health officials fixate possible causes—such as inadequate access to healthcare and other convenience causes—while voiding the potential inconvenient causes that contradict their political narrative.

Our national leaders are enthusiastic supporters of stimulus spending, a Keynsian approach designed to increase demand and stimulate economic growth. When the Bureau of Labor Statistics released its May 2021 inflation numbers, many Democrats and their supporters failed to consider that stimulus spending, which involves expanding the money supply to increase consumer demand, played a potential cause of the higher inflation rate. Activists employ the voiding of the causes strategy when they fail to acknowledge the role resisting arrest plays in deadly encounters between civilians and police. Instead, politicians, activists, and the media fixate on a cause that supports their political narrative. To make a comprehensive analysis, critical thinkers need to establish a chain of causation to determine why certain events occur. Eliminating one or several links from a chain of causation will lead to inaccurate analysis and faulty thinking.

The law and historical precedence filter:

The United States is a nation of laws, and our nation relies on the rule of law to maintain civil order, a necessary condition for achieving political stability and prosperity. Nations—such as Somalia and Zimbabwe—without the rule of law become failed states.

Our founding fathers bestowed our nation the Bill of Rights, the first ten Amendments to the Constitution, which delineate our rights concerning government. The Bill of Rights protects us against a tyrannical government, the same type of government that rules Venezuela and North Korea.

The First Amendment guarantees free speech, the right to assemble peaceably, and the right to petition the government. Whenever we see a protest march on television, we must consider the bill of rights before supporting government action that violates protesters' rights. We must also respect the right of people to share unpopular, distasteful, and offensive opinions before we cancel them and banish them to political purgatory.

We elect legislators and congresspersons to write laws. When politicians write laws that we do not like, then we should vote them out of office. In theory, the government does not allow us to choose which laws we support and which laws we do not support. Such as we ask jurors to decide cases based on the law, not what the law should be. We also ask jurors to set aside their biases and only consider the facts of the case. A jury panel that fails to adhere to these principles is essentially subscribing to mob rule. Whenever we analyze ideas and interpret events, we must always consider the law and legal precedence.

We must also consider historical precedence when analyzing ideas and events. Today in the United States, fringe groups—such as Antifa, the Communist Party of the USA, and the Revolutionary Communist Party—ignore past communist atrocities. These misguided revolutionaries believe they can implement communism better than the founding thought-leaders and the original implementers of communism. These purveyors of misguided utopian ideology have failed to the lessons of history. Racist organizations —such as the KKK, Aryan Nation, and White Aryan Resistance— fail to acknowledge the past atrocities groups like their's have imposed on Americans throughout our history.

The United States is facing a crime wave, a crime wave similar to the one we faced in the 1970s and 80s. During the 1960s, the criminal justice pendulum swung from a more punitive approach to a less punitive approach to addressing crime. Though the proponents of de-policing and de-incarceration are well-intentioned, we cannot systemically change criminal justice policies without testing these policies at a smaller scale, following a more scientific approach that seeks to determine the efficaciousness of these new policies before implementing them on a broader scale. For example, a city cannot simply slash a police department budget without a methodical planning and evaluation process to measure the efficacy of any new proposal. A wise city council might wait until the data is from other cities before implementing new, draconian policies.

Making matters worse, district attorneys—such as Chesa Boudin of San Francisco and George Gascon of Los Angeles might evaluate past practices that led to historically high crime rates before systematically changing criminal justice policies that might produce the same historically high crime rates of the 1970s. The misguided criminal justice philosophy of New York City Mayor De Blasio is likely to bring about the same high crime rates that drove the plotlines of various 1970s-era crime dramas that depict a filthy, crime-ridden New York City. The United States needs wise politicians and their supporters to examine and evaluate historical practices before implementing the same policies that failed in the past.

The hyper-partisan media and politicians often criticize their political opponents for committing the same harmful acts that their side committed in the past. Republicans in Congress seem to ignore deficits when there is a Republican president; they are hypercritical of deficits when the president is a Democrat. As a result, Republican voters incessantly criticize Democrats for excessive spending while ignoring excessive spending under a Republican president. Hypercritical voters should contextualize their arguments regarding deficit spending by acknowledging their side's historical mistakes in the past, providing their argument greater credibility.

The media produced stories that implied that President Trump constructed "cages" on the southern border to house migrants crossing illegally into the United States to discredit the embattled president. The media failed to add nuance to their criticism of President Trump's immigration policies by ignoring President Obama's immigration policies. While snarky media pundits might call this hypocrisy "whataboutism," it is unfair to judge a particular leader's ideas, policies, and actions without considering the historical precedence established by previous leaders. Critical thinkers can rise above partisan politics by assessing ideas, policies, and actions fairly and free of partisan hypocrisy.

Critical thinkers also consider historical political corruption, such as the Teapot Dome Scandal, Watergate, Savings and Loan Scandal, and other past political scandals, to evaluate politicians' motives for engaging in certain activities. For example, the Watergate scandal teaches us that politicians will violate their voters' trust and oath of office to save their political careers. When law enforcement and the media implicate a particular politician who committed a crime, voters need to analyze the politicians' behavior through a historical lens. If other politicians have committed the same crimes in the past, it is not outside the possibility for current politicians to commit the same crimes. This analysis does not impugn the accused politician, however. Instead, this analysis provides context to determine the possible motive.

For example, the media failed to consider Hilary Clinton's motives for hiring a Fusion GPS to conduct opposition research on presidential candidate Trump, which led to the miscredited Russian collusion hoax. History may not always repeat itself, but we can compare current political events with past events. In Hilary Clinton's case, there are enough similarities between her involvement in the Russian collusion hoax and President Nixon's involvement in the Watergate scandal to warrant greater scrutiny of media scrutiny.

The social psychology theories and laws of human nature filter:

Though many of the theories in psychology are controversial—such as Freud's theory of psychosexual development—many of these controversial theories are tantalizingly applicable in today's world. Analytical thinkers can apply these theories to make sense of human behavior and help us understand how people think.

Analyzing our current political climate through the social psychology lens provides us an in-depth analysis of why our political climate seems to be deteriorating. The United States is Balkanizing, representing a divided nation in which each side is ensconced in an ideology that radically opposes the other side. The leftists' embrace of socialism, nationalistic ideology, and identity politics are hastening this division. With the identity politics spreading throughout the United States like a virus, some Americans seek ideological refuge in fringe groups. Without a sense of belongingness, purpose, and identity, rudderless Americans yearn for a sense of belongingness, identity, and purpose by joining groups like Patriot Prayer, Proud Boys, Antifa, and Black Lives Matter. Our social identity, the "we" aspect of who we are, emanates from our group memberships. Hence, one cannot arrive at a complete or even adequate analysis of various political ideas or inflammatory events without considering human behavior and how people interact.

We know that people tend to attribute a person's behavior to internal dispositions and fail to consider situational dispositions (the fundamental attribution error). Analytical thinkers can apply the fundamental attribution error when analyzing police shootings and racially charged events involving so-called "Karens" before forming opinions. Furthermore, we should consider availability heuristics before determining the severity of a problem. Availability heuristics explain why powerful anecdotes can be more provocative than mere statistical evidence. For example, we know that rare events—such as shark attacks and Islamic terrorist attacks—are rare.

Nevertheless, we allow the media's incessant coverage of these rare but sensational events to foment fear, anger, and a desire to act. Though the police kill approximately fifteen unarmed African Americans per year, the media's constant coverage of these events makes them readily available in our memory, making us believe they are more prevalent than they are. When the media constantly aired video of the two airliners crashing into the World Trade Center towers, Americans must have felt like they were under constant attack by Al-Qaeda terrorists. Therefore, we must analyze news stories through the availability heuristics component of the social psychology filter before determining the severity of a particular problem addressed by the media.

By applying the in-group/outgroup tool analysis tool to our current political situation, an analytical thinker might conclude that human nature motivates us to join groups the reflect our values. This desire to be a group member enhances our survivability through the "safety in numbers doctrine." Once we are group members with like-minded people who share our values and goals, we tend to view members of our group (the in-group) favorably and members of the other group (out-group) unfavorably. Since this desire to join groups is instinctual, we will not decode this behavior from our DNA anytime soon. Unfortunately, nefarious leaders will always exploit this undeniable fact for their political advantage. Therefore, voters need to analyze ideas and events with this concept in mind.

Consequently, any leader aspiring to ameliorate our current political climate can gain insight through Muzafer Sherif's famous Robbers Cave experiment, concluding that intergroup conflict occurs when groups compete for scarce resources. The famous experiment offers hope, however. A superordinate goal—such as repelling an alien invasion—can unite rival factions.

While the history and legal precedence filters alert us that an event has happened (police shooting) and similar events have happened in the past, social psychology provides possible explanations of why certain events are happening in the present. Thus, analytical people should filter any events involving human interactions through the social psychology filter to develop an in-depth, comprehensive analysis before concluding.

The philosophical beliefs filter:

When most of us debate people with different political views, we probably assume they possess the same liberal values foundational in the United States Constitution. We assume our well-intentioned adversaries believe in the scientific method, reasoning, democratic values, and capitalism. We also believe that our political adversaries share common values, common goals, and standard methods for making sense of the world with fellow Americans, even if we disagree with their politics. We believe that we can persuade our adversaries through logic, reasoning, and facts. This mistake of believing that everyone shares our philosophical worldview and using logic, reasoning, and facts to win debates causes the liberal-minded not to understand our current political climate.

For example, Antifa continues to promote chaos in Portland and other cities around the country. To those who do not understand the philosophical movement that animates Antifa and their media and political apologists, Antifa consists of idealistic young Americans who aspire to defeat fascism in the United States. We assume that Antifa members share our appreciation for democracy and capitalism and fight fascism to protect America's values and institutions. This assumption is wrong, however. Antifa followers support anarcho-communism, an ideology that seeks to destroy leadership hierarchies. These misguided Americans also believe in collectivism, eliminating private property. Therefore, they do not support the same Enlightenment values that unite our nation. Hence, one cannot sufficiently analyze Antifa's actions without evaluating these actions through the philosophical beliefs filter.

Over the past three hundred-plus years, the Enlightenment values have shaped scientific, political, social, and economic thought worldwide. The Enlightenment thinkers elevated reasoning over mysticism, capitalism over feudalism, and liberalism over tyranny. Humankind's significant progress in science, governance, and economics has proven the superiority of Enlightenment philosophy over the past three hundred years. However, despite our significant progress, politicians, academics, activists, and other nefarious, intellectually dishonest actors attempt to overthrow established order and replace it with a new philosophical system —postmodernism, a philosophical system that rejects Enlightenment values.

Professor Stephen Hicks, Canadian-American philosopher, Professor Jordan Peterson, psychologist, and others delineate the postmodern movement that has swept through the universities since the 1960s. According to Professor Hicks, postmodern philosophers, and their adherents, believe "we live today in the dim ruins of the Enlightenment project, which was the ruling project of the modern period." (https://www.youtube.com/watch?v=-BGbHG63x8w) Postmodern philosophers reject grand narratives that support republican forms of government and capitalist systems. Postmodernists are also skeptical about the human capacity for knowledge and reasoning, believing that truth and knowledge are meaningless concepts, according to Professor Hicks. Furthermore, postmodernists believe the powerful among us create language to create knowledge, and they use that knowledge to wield power, making language and knowledge subjective and not objective. According to postmodern philosophers, the absence of knowledge, objective truth, and reasoning allows us to define our truth, explaining why certain activists champion lived experience arguments over objective truth and facts.

The bad ideas that many politicians and activists espouse today typically do not manifest from the abyss. These radical ideas for fundamentally transforming the United States emanate from postmodern philosophy. Furthermore, one does not have to be a conspiracy theorist to recognize evidence of postmodern ideology deriving from politicians and activists. Politicians and activists use postmodern rhetoric to redefine the political narrative, inspiring political activism. Politicians and activists use intersectionality, identity politics, and equity to influence the political narrative to overturn the leadership hierarchies to gain power in the United States. One has to follow the money and see who benefits from this philosophical and political power-grab ripping the country apart on racial, ethnic, gender, religious, and political lines. According to Stephen Hicks, power is the only game in town in the minds of postmodernists. People who subscribe to postmodernism seem to reject the role competence plays in leadership hierarchies; instead, they believe that organizations build their hierarchies on power alone. The American project has worked well for over two hundred years because our system incentives competent people to rise to the top of leadership hierarchies, allowing everyone to benefit from their contributions to society. Hence, critical thinkers should filter governmental policies through the philosophical beliefs filter before agreeing to policy changes that fundamentally transform our government into a failed state.

CHAPTER 2: HOW WE GOT HERE!

Americans live in perilous times, and the divisive nature of our politics places the United States on a collision course with political, economic, and social disaster. The path to our current state of divisiveness began long before the inauguration of Donald Trump. The current war between the Democratic Party and the Republican Party arguably began during the Robert Bork Supreme Court confirmation hearings in 1987.

In 1998, Republicans intensified their partisan war between the two parties by impeaching President Clinton. A few years later, President Bush's narrow victory over Vice President Gore in 2000 amplified feelings of hostility, suspicion, and hatred between Democrats and Republicans. The vitriol between the two parties would continue through the presidencies of George W. Bush, Barack Obama, and Donald Trump, with no end in sight as we navigate through the early stages of the Biden Administration. Conservative, left-wing media and social media will undoubtedly continue to fan the flames of political division in the United States.

In 2004, Mark Zuckerberg launched Facebook, forever changing political discourse, news distribution, and media consumption in the United States and worldwide. Zuckerberg carefully designed Facebook to activate the brain's reward system by giving us a dopamine high for every "like" and validating comment we receive. Once Facebook created its newsfeed, news outlets began using Facebook to distribute their stories, allowing news organizations to turn salacious stories into clickbait to generate likes and reposts, generating substantial profits for beleaguered news organizations. With fewer people watching network news and reading print media, news organizations discovered a new method for attracting customers.

Before the Internet and the launch of Facebook, printed news stories proliferated based on subscribers' numbers. Television news stories relied on the news story's initial broadcast ratings. Television news stories typically died after they initially aired. Thanks to Facebook, however, salacious and partisan news stories never die; they live for eternity, reverberating through our partisan echo chambers as Facebook continues to feed our insatiable appetites for news that supports our worldviews.

In 2006, when Facebook started taking off, Jack Dorsey launched Twitter—providing another news, information, marketing, and distribution platform for corporations, self-promotors, political partisans, and news organizations. Jack Dorsey, like Mark Zucker-berg, designed Twitter to activate the brain's reward system, pro-viding politicians, activists, media representatives a platform to promote their ideas with clickbait. The media use clickbait to provoke an emotional reaction, thus causing anger and outrage over a salacious story. This anger and outrage motivate partisans to repost these stories in their social media echo chambers. As Facebook and Twitter's popularity grew, Americans became more divided by the political ranker promoted by Facebook and Twitter.

Donald Trump's shocking victory over Hilary Clinton induced mass hysteria among angry Democrats. Fueled by President Trump's inarticulate comments and tweets, many of the presi-dent's angry, young detractors continued to embrace Senator Ber-nie Sanders' brand of left-wing populism and academia's strain of identity politics and post-modernism, fueling political and social unrest in our cities.

Americans are at ideological odds with each other. For Democrats, that ideological narrative encompasses social justice and the government's role in distributing resources and ensuring equality of outcomes for all Americans. For Republicans, that ideological narrative encompasses personal responsibility and the government's role in protecting individual liberties. Though their ideological narratives seem simple enough, the two parties have drifted further apart ideologically.

Anyone who knows about street gangs knows that gangs typically identify themselves through colors and symbols. For example, the Bloods street gang identifies with red; the Crips street gang identifies with blue. Terrorist organizations—such as the KKK, Antifa, Aryan Nation, Al-Qaeda, and ISIS use colors and symbols to promote group identity and unity. Our two political parties work the same way: The Republicans identify with red; the elephant symbolizes the Republican Party. The Democrats identify with blue; the donkey symbolizes the Democratic Party. The two parties, the reds and the blues are essentially in the midst of a gang war, fighting on social media, in the streets, and at the ballot box. This gang mentality that is permeating our politics should not surprise anyone. Our social media habits fuel this war, and Mark Zuckerberg and Jack Dorsey are the two prominent generals leading this dangerous and destructive battle.

People immerse themselves in rancorous partisan politics for the same reasons young people join street gangs: to indulge in self-righteous fantasies relating to power and dominance, for a sense of purpose, for a sense of belonging, and to channel negative energies toward the outgroup (members of the opposing party). Partisans invade the streets as if they are fighting for turf. They wear their colors (red or blue); they wave their banners, antagonizing each other like a less-than-charming version of Westside Story. Nevertheless, there are explanations for all this madness. Many of the concepts from social psychology explain why we witness what we see in our world of politics.

The media sensationalize specific news stories to generate fear and anger among partisans on both sides of the fight. When these sensational stories go viral, they often attract significant attention to partisan news channels—such as Fox News, MSNB, CNN, and other news outlets. From there, angry partisans post these salacious news stories in their social media echo chambers, generating millions of reposts worldwide. Rare events-such as the police shootings of unarmed African Americans—often attract significant media attention because they are rare, creating the perception that these events are more common than they are. The media's constant, ubiquitous coverage makes the information more readily available in our memory. The media's failure to report these stories with greater context promotes anger, fear, and mistrust within the nation. As consumers of the media, we need to be less reactive and wait for the facts when these stories go viral.

People form into groups for various reasons: safety, a sense of belonging, a sense of identity, and purpose. Often these groups compete for scarce resources—such as prizes (gameshows like Survivor), grants (nonprofits and NGOs), wins (sports teams), natural resources (countries), and votes (politicians). When running for office, politicians are competing for votes; when politicians win their elections, they compete for positions on influential committees; once they become well-known, they punch their ticket and move up to the next highest office (the US Senate or the presidency). While they are in office, they do everything necessary to acquire party dominance. Thus, the party that wins most of these limited positions can distribute scarce resources to those who finance their campaign victories: wealthy donors and constituents. Once in office, politicians in both parties do everything necessary to stay in power. In the process, both parties use tactics that cause their supporters to hate the other party's supporters. Both parties deploy this cynical strategy to deflect blame and anger away from them.

The politicians do not directly attack the voters, however. They encourage their voters to do the attacking, essentially turning the voters against each other. Therefore, the elites with power and privilege have convinced angry partisans without power and privilege that partisans without power and privilege are causing America's problems. For example, Democrats seem to direct their anger toward the poor, uneducated, and out-of-work coal miners who self-medicate with opioids to mask their psychic pain in the Appalachians.

Instead of the voters being angry at a career politician's support for the ill-advised and ill-conceived Iraq war and the Libyan air campaign, the voters are mad at each other. Instead of being angry over the privilege that the rich and powerful enjoy, voters are mad at other voters who do not share the same advantages as elites. Nancy Pelosi can gobble up expensive ice cream, and Gavin Newsome can dine at the ultra-expensive French restaurant while protesters blame our country's problems on hardworking working-class and middle-class Americans who are just trying to pay their bills. The politicians want it this way; they would rather have the voters fighting amongst each other instead of fighting to remove them from office. Unfortunately, American politicians and their constituents are doing our enemies' bidding.

In the 2002 movie "The Sum of all Fears," a political thriller starring Ben Affleck as Jack Ryan and Morgan Freeman as Director of the CIA, neofascists devise a plan to turn the United States against Russia, provoking a nuclear war that destroys both superpowers and creating a power vacuum for the neofascists to fill. Through the use of fear and mistrust, the neofascist mastermind nearly goads the United States and Russia into a nuclear war. In the end, CIA analyst Jack Ryan staves off disaster by reestablishing communication and trust between the United States and Russia. This plot should sound familiar, except our enemies are goading the Russians to destroy us; instead, they inspire us to destroy ourselves.

The Russians, Chinese Communist Party, Iranians, Venezuelans, and North Koreans must be pleased over the United States' political chaos. If Russia and the Chinese Communist Party are trying to sow the seeds of turmoil in the United States, our politicians and voters seem happy to help these two nefarious governments accomplish their goals. However, any rational country would not give another country the power to foment revolution within its borders, but American politicians and voters do not appear sensible these days. Russia and China have realized that they do not have to destroy America with nuclear missiles; they can persuade America to destroy itself, allowing Russia and China to fill the power vacuum. Today, we need goodwill leaders to establish communication and trust between both parties and not acquiesce to Russia and China's goal of destroying America.

For the last four years, Democrats have blamed Russia for stealing the 2016 election for President Trump. The close results from the 2020 presidential election invited allegations of foreign interference from China and other nefarious actors. If these allegations of foreign interference are true, then American leaders need to wake up. Donald Trump, Nancy Pelosi, Chuck Schumer, Mitch McConnell, and others need to stop playing into the hands of America's enemies. Our leaders need to unite to fight this foreign threat to America's sovereignty and well-being. Unfortunately, our two parties are busy destroying each other to appreciate what is happening to our dysfunctional political system. Since our politicians seem unwilling to address this threat, grassroots leaders need to rise to fight the two-party system's dysfunction.

We need leaders to emerge who recognize that the United States can address America's problems without abandoning the United States constitution. We also need leaders who acknowledge that we can address income inequality and the widening gap between our wealthy elites and the middle class and poor without abandoning capitalism, recognize the value that both liberals and conservatives bring to the political debate, that there are conservative solutions to liberal problems and liberal solutions to traditional problems.

CHAPTER 3: GOVERNING CONCEPTS

For the two political parties to overcome this ideological stalemate, we need a new movement to emerge that allows the two political parties to eschew petty partisan politics for the sake of our nation's future. America needs political leaders who can transcend partisan politics' narrow ideological confines to save the country from a sociopolitical civil war.

Brett Weinstein—the Evergreen College professor who resigned after challenging Evergreen's 'Day of Absence protest —launched a movement in the summer of 2020 to challenge two-party rule the "duopoly" (a term that professor Weinstein uses to describe our two-party system) (https://www.nytimes.com/2017/06/01/opinion/when-the-left-turns-on-its-own.html).   To professor Weinstein and other thought leaders from the Intellectual Dark Web, it is painfully apparent that the United States cannot survive a sociopolitical civil war. When two elephants fight, the grass suffers.

Professor Weinstein's Unity Project seeks to unite disaffected Democrats and Republicans, wary of partisan warfare, by recruiting a patriotic Republican and Democrat to form a bipartisan ticket for president/vice president. This bipartisan ticket would agree to manage the United States government's executive branch as a team, providing a voice for both sides of the political divide while stripping power from the party elites who prosper from this divisive nature of partisan politics.

The unity ticket would need to build a party platform that addresses problems that animate both liberals and conservatives to govern effectively. Unity Party supporters would need to abandon party orthodoxy to identify and implement policies that address current issues in our country for the unity ticket to work. This heterodox strategy would allow our leaders to adopt policies from both sides of the political debate.

Additionally, the Unity Party would need to collaborate with Democratic Party leaders and Republican Party leaders to reduce the vitriolic rhetoric emanating from both sides. Like the old days, our politicians would need to resolve issues over cocktails; they would also need to agree to reduce the ad hominem attacks on each other, serving as role models for their constituents to have a civilized yet lively debate. The late Senator John McCain's defense of then-Senator Barack Obama during the 2008 presidential campaign serves as an example of how political opponents should treat each other.

Liberals would need to acknowledge the unintended consequences that result from the rapid, untested, and systematic implementation of policies and programs that produce more significant problems than they intend to solve. Conservatives would need to acknowledge benignly neglecting issues that animate progressives would fuel political discontent and unrest.

The former Democratic leaders and former Republican leaders of the Unity Party would need to adhere to a new philosophy that is pragmatic for these difficult political times. Moreover, this newly created Unity Party would need to implement policies that address problems that threaten our country's stability. Here is a list of policy proposals the Unity Party should adopt for its party platform:

1. **Strengthen America's social contract:** The United States cannot survive and thrive without a robust social

contract that unites all Americans regardless of race, ethnicity, national origins, religion, gender, and political ideology. The United States will not continue to prosper if America cannot unite behind shared values and interests. American citizens will not fulfill their patriotic obligations if trust in the American system and faith in fellow Americans disintegrate. Americans will no longer fight for a country they no longer support. Americans will avoid paying taxes to a government that fails to represent their values and interests. Americans will no longer believe in the rule of law if the government no longer applies the rule of law equally.

According to the doctrine of original sin, every person born is morally corrupt, and it is beyond human capacity to overcome this evil nature without God rescuing us from our "sinful" behaviors. For those who believe that God grants us free will, there is no denying that many humans will indulge in self-serving, destructive behavior in the pursuit of power and pleasure, which promote the individual's survival, often at the expense of the group. This self-serving behavior makes collectivism a less pragmatic strategy considering how mother nature wires the brain to favor the individual's survival. After all, Adam Smith, the great 18th-century economist, argued that society could achieve its best results when individuals are free to pursue their interests.

Those who do not believe in God and the doctrine of original sin can probably agree that humans are born with bad-tempered behavior encoded in our DNA, and it is beyond human capacity to overcome this bad-tempered behavior through any level of social engineering. Thus, there is no escaping the fact that our flawed nature prohibits us from creating a utopian paradise with wise, temperate, and noble leaders capable of overcoming self-serving impulses to the benefit of those governed. The best we can do is create a government that strikes the correct balance between protecting us from each other and those who rule over us. To achieve this proper balance, citizens must agree to a social contract that considers individual rights and responsibilities that takes human nature and psychology into consideration.

In the state of nature, the instinct to survive and propagate drives humans to fight to conquer their environment and dominate other humans. This quest to conquer and dominate elevates the strongest, most competent humans to the top of the dominance hierarchy, which promotes and enhances one's survivability and, in many cases, enhances the group's survivability. Unfortunately, this quest for power often elevates cruel, incompetent humans to the top of the dominance hierarchy, resulting in "dystopian dictatorships" that violate human rights and individual freedoms. Leaders of these dystopian dictatorships often rise to power by promising to produce the perfect egalitarian society, a society of total equality (equity). The ambitious among us, those who have sociopathic and narcissistic tendencies, use their charisma, status, and privilege to pursue paths toward power. These sociopathic and narcissistic politicians often recycle discredited past ideologies, repackage them, and sell them to a new generation of naïve, idealist adherents looking for a new revolution to fight. Unfortunately, these naïve, idealistic adherents fail to learn lessons from the past.

Naïve Americans commit the fallacy of infallibility when they believe the United States has progressed beyond the point of regression, meaning we have learned our lessons from the past, and we are above making the same mistakes as past societies. When the fallacy of infallibility establishes itself in the collective mindset of citizens of advanced empires, such as Rome, England, and the United States, citizens believe their nation is incapable of making the same mistakes that have destroyed past empires. Americans also commit the fallacy of infallibility when they believe that America is immune to the same problems that make third-world countries ungovernable. For example, hyperinflation destroyed Venezuela, Zimbabwe, and the Weimar Republic. Today's Democratic politicians seem to think America is immune to the same hyperinflation that destroyed these nations. Also, those of us who support critical race theory seem to believe that America is incapable of fragmenting like Yugoslavia and post-invasion Iraq. What must wonder whether a nation can survive when its citizens form into identity groups.

Hubris has caused several nations to abandon or reject capitalism in favor of communism, despite communism's dismal record. Communist enthusiasts often argue that "communism has never worked because no one has implemented it correctly." Those who believe this "blame-the-jockey-but-not-the-horse" argument neglect to acknowledge that communism ignores human nature and historical precedence. After the communist Soviet empire's catastrophic failure, no sane intellectual should have promoted communism again in our universities. Unfortunately, our leftist intellectuals ignored the stacks of dead bodies that communism has wrought.

Historians often refer to World War I as the "war that ended all wars." Since World War I was so horrible, political leaders worldwide believed that no nation would want to fight another war as horrific—then World War II started in 1939. During World War II, war atrocities transcended the battle-field. Upon Germany's surrender, allied commanders exposed the horrors of the Holocaust. After the world learned about Germany's crimes against humanity, world leaders said, "never again." Unfortunately, genocides continued to occur: The communist Khmer Rouge slaughtered hundreds of thousands of Cambodians in the 1970s; Rwanda's majority Hutu population slaughtered thousands of Tutsis 1990s. George Santayana famously stated, "Those who cannot remember the past are condemned to repeat it." Santayana's quote reminds us of our fallibility and stubborn unwillingness to learn lessons from our historical misdeeds.

According to the late Aleksandr Solzhenitsyn, "But the line dividing good and evil cuts through the heart of every human being. And who is willing to destroy a piece of his own heart?" Since human behavior's destructive elements are within us all, we can expect the same tragic mistakes to continue throughout human history. Those who believe that humans are too civilized or advanced to repeat the same grievous errors of the past fail to acknowledge the destructive instincts that reside within us all, instincts we inherit from our ancestors dating back to the beginning of human history.

According to the late psychologist Carl Jung, the collective unconscious consists of our unconscious memories and impulses that reside within us all. We inherit these collective memories and urges from our ancestors dating back to the beginning of time. Our collective unconscious contains archetypes, which are elemental images or ideals that live within us all, making us all capable of being both heroes—like Joan of Arc, Martin Luther King, and Malala Yousafzai—and villains—like Adolph Hitler, Saddam Hussein. Suppose we are to subscribe to Jung's collective unconscious theory. In that case, we can suspect that these villains live among us, waiting for the right circumstances to unleash their tyrannical impulses on a politically and socially unstable nation thirsting for a leader who promises to lead its citizens toward a utopian paradise.

Without proper vigilance and self-awareness, the villain can undermine the values that unite us all, causing the next Joseph Stalin, Adolph Hitler, Fidel Castro, Hugo Chavez, or Pol Pot to emerge. To inoculate ourselves from utopian revolutionary fervor, Americans must cherish and protect the canons that unite us and protect us from the corrupting influences that can destroy us all.

To live successfully in groups, we must build a civilized society organized around a social contract. The social contract is an agreement between members within a community or group (cities, states, and national governments) that dictates how we organize our government (monarchy, democracy, republican form of government, socialism, capitalism, or communism). The rule of law is the central element of any social contract. The rule of law is essentially the glue that unites society. Lamentably, societies tend to fail when the rule of law disintegrates, hurtling us toward a state of nature where anarchy and chaos reign.

For thousands of years, humankind lived in a static state. Worldwide conditions had barely advanced beyond the state of nature. Technology advanced rapidly, life expectancy increased gradually, and the human condition improved at a nominal rate. Then the Enlightenment arrived. The great Enlightenment philosophers, such as John Locke, Rene Descartes, and others, gifted the world a set of values and governing principles that ushered in the modernity era for the western world and eventually for many parts of the nonwestern world. The Enlightenment values of individual freedom, democratic ideals, and capitalism revolutionized politics and economics, improving the quality of life and living standards for generations worldwide.

Based on reasoning and objective truth, Enlightenment philosophy gave birth to the scientific method, which revolutionized science, technology, and medicine. What is more, the great Enlightenment served as a foundational value system that eventually improved the quality of life, as evidenced by advances in technology, increases in life expectancy, and reduced global poverty.

Locke and Descartes's Enlightenment philosophy created the most extraordinary country ever, the United States, to serve as a beacon of hope and opportunity for those who wish to share the nation's values. The nation's founding fathers created a near-perfect government with a robust social contract that would unite generations of future Americans in striving to create a more perfect union, articulated in President Lincoln's "Emancipation Proclamation" and Dr. King's "I Have a Dream Speech."

To this day, the United States is not a perfect country; however, no country is perfect because humans are born in a state of original sin, or, in secular terms, we are born with instincts and drives that can corrupt us all. Therefore, sinful or corruptible people will always make an imperfect government. The flaws that are minimally inherent in our government system are inherent in all government systems. Nevertheless, disgruntled and disillusioned Americans impugn the American system without considering the inherent flaws of other government systems throughout the world that devalue individual freedom, discourage technological innovation and progress, and hinder economic opportunity. For instance, leftists often refer to America as being patriarchal and heteronormative. Are there any countries in the world that are not patriarchal or heteronormative?   The world is much better off with the United States in it!

The Enlightenment brought about advances in science, governance, and philosophy that make almost everyone's life better today. Without the Enlightenment, our life expectancy would probably not be much higher than forty. We would probably not enjoy the modern luxuries that help keep us alive and make our lives more comfortable. Even though poverty still prevails today, today's poor have much easier lives than yesterday's rich. Today, poor people would probably not want to relinquish their air condition/heating systems, flat-screen televisions, video game consoles, SUVs, and smartphones to switch places with aristocrats from the 16th century. Most of our nation's poor people own smartphones, which are more powerful than the computers that sent astronauts to the moon. Today's poor have access to virtually all the world's knowledge through smartphones.

Misguided Americans compare our imperfect government with an ideological standard that has never existed and will never exist because humans are deeply flawed and incapable of living mistake-free lives. The type of lives that authoritarians would expect us to live under a utopian system denies the reality of the human condition. Unfortunately, the left's denial of reality encourages some people to believe that we can eliminate bad-tempered behaviors or those urges and drives that enliven the privileged and produce misery and hardship in the lives of those less fortunate.

Well-intentioned social justice activists think that we can create the perfect utopian, egalitarian society devoid of any disparities that animate activists to take to the streets. A strong central government is needed to implement egalitarian principles. Moreover, since autonomy is an inherent value most of us enjoy, a strong central government can only rely on coercion to implement policies disregarding human nature.

President Reagan once said, "Freedom is never more than one generation from extinction," To defend our freedom, Americans must protect the enlightenment values that are the basis of our constitutional government. Therefore, we must protect the social contract to promote unity over tribalism and identity politics. America's robust defense of the social contract will maintain political, economic, and social order for future Americans. To defend our sacred social contract, we must also reject the political opportunists and demagogues among us who wish to promote disunity through disinformation, ranker, division, and chaos. We must be wary of any political movement that seeks to "fundamentally transform" our nation by destroying our social contact and the rule of law.

The social contract compels Americans to respect criminal and civil laws, knowing that our fellow Americans are also doing the same. This agreement between Americans makes us respect others' political views, knowing that our fellow Americans are doing the same. Moreover, the social contract compels us to engage in civic-minded activities, knowing that our fellow Americans are doing the same. Trust and respect between various tribes, factions, or groups can disintegrate when the rule of law evaporates within a country, causing a downward spiral that leads to the destruction of the United States and replacing it with a new postmodern, egalitarian dystopian society.

Postmodernism is an anti-enlightenment philosophy that promotes subjective reality (lived experience) over objective truth. Postmodernism promotes identity politics over nationalism. Postmodernism promotes emotional reasoning (allowing emotions to guide interpretation of reality) over logic and reason; postmodernism rejects grand narratives, such as capitalism, individual sovereignty, and democracy; postmodernism rejects science and the scientific method. In essence, postmodernism rejects Enlightenment values that serve as the foundation of our nation and other western nations worldwide. To usher in a new postmodern society, the thought leaders and political leaders of this nefarious movement need to implement a neo-Marxist strategy that divides people among racial, ethnic, gender, and religious lines. This new movement is implementing a divide and conquer strategy.

Identity politics have quietly swept through our nation's universities over the past fifty years, threatening to divide the country and sow the seeds of chaos wherever those seeds take root, primarily in Democrat-run cities with long histories of poverty and economic stratification.

The rioting in our streets today is not an organic response to the outrageous death of George Floyd. Postmodern professors in American Universities have instilled this revolutionary fervor in our college students over the last fifty years. Consequently, George Floyd's death catalyzed this current anti-enlightenment movement.

Though minor in scale, this new revolutionary movement in the United States seeks to destroy our nation's most sacred compact, our social contract. These unabashed extremists believe they can fill the subsequent power vacuum and create a postmodern, neo-Marxist world that rejects Enlightenment values with the promise of creating an egalitarian society. These postmodern revolutionary leaders must dismantle our institutions and the underlying rights and values that unite our nation to implement this utopian paradise.

The first amendment of the constitution states, "Congress shall make no law respecting an establishment of religion, or prohibiting the free exercise thereof; or abridging the freedom of speech, or the press; or the right of the people peaceably to assemble, and to petition the government for a redress of grievances." Our founding fathers listed this right first for a reason: Protecting this right is fundamental for protecting all other rights. As Americans, we need to protect the rights of our fellow Americans to protest peaceably.

On May 25, 2020, George Floyd died after an encounter with Minneapolis Police. The state accused Minneapolis Police Officer Derek Chauvin of murder. In response to the latest tragedy involving an African American, millions of protestors invaded the streets to register their anger toward a criminal justice system they believe is racist and unjust. Fortunately, most protestors acquitted themselves with dignity and respect. Unfortunately, many nefarious actors from Antifa and the Boogaloo Bois {sic} infiltrated these protests, causing chaos and destroying the lives of those who can least afford to have their lives destroyed. In the end, frustrated

Americans accused big-city mayors of not allowing their police departments to restore law and order. Additionally, some of our big-city district attorneys failed to press charges against the most egregious actors. This failure to enforce the law can have an erosive effect on the rule of law, making compliance arbitrary.

Our inability to respond to COVID is the symptom of a more significant problem: the social contract/the rule of law breakdown. The deterioration of law and order and the arbitrary manner in which public health officials enforce policies have eroded confidence in our political leaders and media, eroding our sense of "we-ness" that united our nation against Nazi Germany and Al-Qaeda. When our leaders—such as Governor Gavin Newsome (California), Speaker Pelosi, and others—refuse to follow their directives, their directives lose their legitimacy. A robust social contract requires citizens to recognize and respect the legitimacy of their leaders. "Lockdown for thee but not for me" is not a legitimate strategy for leaders who want to earn their constituents' trust and respect.

2. **Engage with opposing political viewpoints through motivational interviewing:** Sigmund Freud, the father of modern-day psychology, divided personality into three parts: the id, ego, and superego. The id, according to Freud, operates on the pleasure principle. The id is the part of our personality that consists of our sexual and aggressive drives, causing us to act impulsively. The id operates like a car without brakes. On the other hand, the superego represents the moral principle, which incorporates the values we learn from our caregivers and society. Dopamine, the brain's pleasure chemical, feeds the id's insatiable appetite for pleasure. The superego is the part of our personality that controls the id's impulsive drives. For instance, the superego acts as a shoulder angel, discouraging us from carrying out the impulsive

id's acts. Finally, the ego represents the reality principle. The ego operates on reason. The ego's job is to satisfy the needs of the id without offending the superego. The ubiquity of food, sex, drugs, and technology challenges the ego's job of balancing the pleasure-seeking id. Our tech entrepreneurs and media understand this fact quite well and exploit it to their advantage.

Social media websites, such as Facebook and Twitter, activates the id's aggressive drive through provocative clickbait and overly simplistic memes. Clickbait is an intentionally false, sensational, or misleading headline or prurient picture designed to entice people to click on the associated link. Unfortunately, nefarious actors use clickbait to attract attention and generate outrage in social media echo chambers. Politically biased and often misinformed social media consumers repost this clickbait on their social media newsfeeds, causing this sensationalized information to proliferate around the country and causing more outrage among the masses. Unfortunately, the outrageous news from social media feeds the primal id's insatiable appetite, causing the id part of our personality to return for more biased information that provides the brain's dopamine system instant pleasure.

Making matters worse, the anonymity and lack of human interaction make social media platforms a terrible place to conduct controversial political discussions. The inability to read another person's facial expressions and body language often turn debates on Facebook and Twitter into ad hominin-fueled verbal slugfests, resembling a schoolyard battle between petulant first-graders. Furthermore, these online debates' anonymity often makes it easy to dehumanize the opponent, stripping our political opponents of their humanity as we cast labels on them, such Nazi, racist, leftist, and communist.

Making matters worse, Facebook, YouTube, and other internet websites have developed complex algorithms that allow these purveyors of provocative information to provide consumers steady information that feeds their biased political narratives. Tech moguls, such as Mark Zuckerberg and Jack Dorsey, have amassed enormous wealth by creating social media echo chambers. These echo chambers have caused social media-induced confirmation bias to infect the nation, with fanatics on both ends of the political spectrum trapped in a state of belief perseverance. This belief perseverance stifles respectful political debate as each side becomes further entrenched in its beliefs.

Contrary to what the most ardent defenders of the first amendment might believe, the news media in the United States does not appear to be performing its unofficial role as the fourth branch of government. Though media bias has always been a problem, media bias seems to be more prominent today. In the past, publishers did not have internet and social media to amplify their stories. What used to be a one-time television broadcast can now live forever on YouTube. The most sensational news stories reverberate through social media echo chambers, further stoking outrage among the political partisans. One provocative CNN or Fox News story can generate millions of shares around the world.

Cable news channels seldom disguise their biases. After watching CNN, MSNBC, and Fox News, there is no doubt which candidate they supported in the 2020 presidential campaign. The New York Times editorial page has not endorsed a Republican presidential candidate since President Eisenhower. The Washington Post has not supported a Republican presidential candidate since Jimmy Carter (Patrick Pexton: The Post's endorsements historically tend Democratic - The Washington Post). The Washington Times and New York Post traditionally support Republican candidates and causes. These news outlets feed their partisan consumers' unquenchable appetites, stoking their confirmation bias and belief perseverance.

Our inability to trust media sources that contradict our worldview also causes us to develop belief perseverance (the inability to change our opinions despite contradictory evidence). However, the stubborn unwillingness to accommodate new information does not necessarily cause belief perseverance. Instead, the mistrust of our corrupted news media might be the cause of belief perseverance. The fact that a handful of large corporations own most of our television and print media outlets fuels the belief that much of our news is "fake news," news that supports an ideological, political, social, or corporate narrative, news that reasonable people should not believe.

Since a handful of large, powerful corporations own most media outlets in the United States, it would be reasonable to expect these large news corporations to champion a political narrative that supports their interests. It would also be reasonable to expect groupthink to permeate these new organizations, homogenizing the news that supports certain popular political narratives, feeding outrage, mistrust, and hostility among the citizenry while deflecting scrutiny from the corporate media masters.

Our voracious appetite for biased political information contributes to an outrage culture that has rapidly emerged over the last twenty years. This outrage culture animates the political spectrums' extreme ends, causing people to act in intemperate ways. Terrorist groups—such as neo-Nazis, KKK, various right-wing militias, and Antifa use social media to mobilize like-minded partisans to form outrage mobs, which proliferate online and in the streets. For example, white supremacists and neo-Nazis organized a Unite the Right Rally in Charlottesville, North Carolina, in 2017, which resulted in Heather Heyer's death. A hateful white supremacist drove his car through a crowd of demonstrators, murdering

Heather Heyer.

In 2020, Black Lives Matter and Antifa flooded the streets protesting racism, while Antifa swamped the streets protesting perceived fascism. Nevertheless, it would be intellectually dishonest to place sole blame on social media for animating the disenchanted masses. There are other factors driving discontent, and social media is merely one of those factors, one of which is a lack of leadership from the Democratic and Republican parties. Thus, Americans need to re-evaluate how they consume information on social media or risk fueling a political divide that threatens our constitutional republic. However, there is a model that all of us can follow to lead us out of the political abyss.

Daryl Davis, an African American R&B and Blues musician, became a Ted Talk/YouTube legend by befriending Ku Klux Klan members, ultimately activating these KKK members' desire to renounce their racist views and quit the organization. According to Davis's website, "Davis consistently approaches each of his subjects as individuals; some he comes to respect and even like."

Davis's strategy is simple: He listens to people without guilting them, shaming them, judging, and threatening them, resisting the feelings of sanctimony and self-righteousness that might prevent most of us from having difficult conversations with people we oppose politically. In The Guardian, Davis claims "these KKK members convert themselves (https://www.theguardian.com/music/2020/mar/18/daryl-davis-black-musician-who-converts-ku-klux-klan-members)." In a Ted Talk (https://www.bing.com/videos/search?q=daryl+davis+ted +talk&&view=detail&mid=816713A356CB7AF77C2D81671 3A356CB7AF77C2D&&FORM=VRDGAR&ru=%2Fvideos %2Fsearch%3Fq%3Ddaryl%2Bdavis%2Bted%2Btalk %26FORM%3DHDRSC4),

https://www.youtube.com/watch?
v=IH1lh_iR70w&has_verified=1&bpctr=1606783880),
Davis says, "Respect is the key, sitting down and talking; not necessarily agreeing, respecting each other to air their views (sic)." Davis further implores his audience to "Take the time to talk to your adversaries," which is good advice for partisans on both ends of the political divide.

Motivational interviewing (MI), developed by William R. Miller and Stephen Rollnick, is a counseling style designed to activate a person's motivation for changing their behavior. MI practitioners avoid judging, blaming, or criticizing their clients; instead, they use some of Daryl Davis's same strategies when he speaks with Ku, Klux, Klan members.

When practicing MI, counselors strategically use four skills —open-ended questions, affirmations, reflections, and summaries to activate a person's reasons for changing their behavior. MI practitioners skillfully use reflective listening when counseling their clients. When MI practitioners use reflective listening, they are sending the following message to their clients: "Everything that you are saying is important, and my goal is to see the world through your eyes to gain a deeper understanding of you." In essence, MI is non-confrontational and non-coercive. MI practitioners never offer advice or try to convince their clients to change; instead, MI practitioners use their skills to guide their clients toward change without confronting them.

To facilitate productive debates like to change opinions, we should consider following a non-confrontational approach and employing MI strategies to guide our political opponents toward consensus. The opposite approach, demonstrated by rightwing and leftwing extremist groups, does not work, however. It is counter-productive for members of Antifa and Patriot Prayer to yell at each other.

The 2020 Black Lives Matter/Antifa protests prove one theory: Browbeating, shaming, and threatening people with opposing views does little to change opinions. When people face coercion from their opponents, they tend to dig in their heels and become even more resistant to changing their views because nobody likes to be wrong. People prefer to discover on their own that their opinions are false.

3. **Acknowledge that we can solve problems only when we identify problems correctly:** Unfortunately, politicians often become trapped within the narrow confines of their ideology when trying to solve problems that animate voters on both ends of the political spectrum. These partisan politicians often analyze problems through an ideological lens that prevents them from identifying a problem correctly, resulting in our government's pervasive inability to solve problems, such as the COVID 19 crisis, efficiently and effectively.

In essence, politicians identify problems in a manner that supports a political narrative. Democrats are guilty of problem misidentification when they identify easy access to guns as "the problem" when easy access to firearms may merely cause a cause of the actual problem: death and injuries resulting from firearms and other violent weapons.

When trying to solve problems, our politicians often commit the fallacy of oversimplification. The Fallacy of oversimplification is the error of taking one single cause of a problem as a complete—or even adequate—explanation of why that problem occurs when, in fact, other significant causes are also operating. In other words, when politicians commit the fallacy of oversimplification, they often focus only on one cause of the problem while ignoring the other causes. When our political leaders commit the fallacy of oversimplification, the problem often goes unresolved.

Drunk driving is a public health problem that results in the death of thousands of people each year. If a city, such as Sacramento, experiences a 100% increase in drunk driving deaths in one year, correctly identifying the problem determines whether the problem is solved. For example, if the Sacramento council claims that there are too many Sacramento bars, then the Sacramento City Council is committing the fallacy of oversimplification. By claiming that having too many bars in Sacramento is the problem, the city council would be identifying a potential cause of drunken driving accidents, having too many bars in the city, as the problem, thus ignoring the other possible causes: lack of enforcement; lenient drunk driving laws; high rates of alcoholism; and cultural attitudes about drinking and driving.

For example, frustrated teachers often identify unmotivated students and apathetic parents as the problem. Republican politicians often identify self-serving teachers' unions as the problem. On the other hand, Democratic politicians often identify a lack of money as the problem. Students often identify boring teachers and uninteresting curriculum as the problem. Parents often blame lazy teachers as the problem. In the previous examples, the teachers, politicians, parents, and students commit the fallacy of oversimplification.

Let us say the Democratic politicians are correct—that a lack of money is the problem. If the government doubles, triples, or even quadruples education spending, the education system will probably not produce better results. By focusing on one aspect of a single cause of the problem (lack of money), we would be ignoring the other possible causes of the problem: lazy, disinterested students, lack of school choice, lazy, poorly trained teachers, boring, irrelevant curriculum, and other possible causes. Therefore, the actual problem relating to education is low literacy rates, low test scores, and low graduation rates, in other words, poor education outcomes.

Politicians need to be intellectually honest enough to avoid allowing political ideology to contaminate the problem identification process to prevent committing the fallacy of over-simplification. In other words, politicians should avoid defining problems to fit certain political narratives.

Also, politicians can apply the "why test" during the problem identification process to avoid committing the fallacy of oversimplification. During the problem identification process, politicians can use the "why test" to the problem statement: Why are too many bars the problem? Too many bars are the problem because people drink, drive, and cause accidents that injure and kill people when they leave bars; therefore, injuries and death are the problems, not guns.

4. **Consider the law of unintended consequences before passing new laws and implementing new policies:** According to the old proverb, "The road to hell is paved with good intentions." Wise leaders understand that excellent intentions are not enough to solve problems. Wise people understand that some problems have no solutions, and the solutions for some problems are so costly that trying to solve them merely produces unintended consequences that are far greater than the problem that we are attempting to solve.

According to the great American economist Dr. Thomas Sowell, "There are no solutions; there are only trade-offs (https://www.goodreads.com/book/show/3047.A_Conflict_of_Visions). For example, to respond to the COVID 19 crisis, politicians traded middle and working-class Americans' economic security for health and safety, creating unintended consequences—such as increasing financial hardship, suicides, and drug overdoses.

According to the law of unintended consequences, when we try to solve problems, we sometimes create more significant problems for individuals and society as a whole. Hence, impulsive politicians produce unintended consequences through their ill-conceived policies, trapping themselves in tier one thinking, which is the inability to consider cause and effect. It is as if these near-sighted politicians cannot project into the future. We have seen this happen numerous times throughout history. For example, Adolph Hitler seemed oblivious to the ramifications behind waging war against Russia during World War 2. His ill-conceived strategies and tactics caused many German soldiers to die in Russia while pinning his military down in a two-front war.

Our DNA harbors a significant desire to solve problems. Without this desire to solve problems, human progress would have seized thousands of years ago, and we would probably still be living in caves without the amenities that make life easier. Moreover, the brain's dopamine reward system provides us a natural high when we do things essential for our survival, and solving problems is vital for our survival.

Modern-day problem-solvers often obtain patent rights, build large businesses, accumulate vast wealth, and win prestigious prizes. Problem-solvers tend to advance through the competence hierarchy, earning significant status, wealth, and prestige, earning a dopamine high throughout the process.

Voters often malign politicians for problems they cannot control, making politicians desperate when significant problems occur. For example, the United States, Israel, and other allies in the Middle East and worldwide considered Iraq's late dictator, Saddam Hussein, a national security problem. The United States and its allies accused Saddam of harboring weapons of mass destruction program, threatening regional and global security. In response, the international community imposed a WMD inspection program on Iraq. When

Saddam failed to cooperate fully with United Nations weapons inspectors, the Bush administration used faulty intelligence to justify a full-scale war against Iraq.

The Bush Administration's neoconservatives convinced Hillary Clinton, other Democratic leaders, and the media that the only way to solve the Saddam problem was to wage war against Iraq. On March 19, 2003, the United States and its allies launched a major air campaign against Iraq, initiating one of the longest wars in United States history.

America's inability to find weapons of mass destruction delegitimized the war in the minds of many. Tragically, the Bush Administration's overthrow of the dictatorial Saddam Hussein produced unintended consequences that resulted in worse problems than the war resolved. The United States lost nearly 5,000 soldiers and paid almost $2 trillion, which the United States could have used to rebuild our nation's infrastructure.

Before the Iraq War, the Sunni-dominated Iraqi government served as a counterbalance to the Shiite-dominated Iranian regime. After the war, the Iranian Revolutionary guard moved into Iraq, threatening its balance of power. Moreover, when the United States drew down its military forces, the ISIS terrorist organization moved in, capturing thirty percent of Syria and forty percent of Iraq according to the Wilson Center (Timeline: the Rise, Spread, and Fall of the Islamic State | Wilson Center). Furthermore, despite spending nearly $2 trillion on the Iraq war, the United States is arguably no better off today from a national security perspective. With Iran poised to acquire nuclear weapons in the future, the United States government will undoubtedly continue to fight in proxy wars throughout the Middle East, costing American lives and degrading our military's ability to face real threats such as China. Unfortunately, President Obama made a similar mistake when he authorized a major air campaign against Libyan dictator, Muammar Gaddafi, resulting in Libya becoming a failed terrorist state. Had the Obama Administration considered the possible unintended consequences more carefully, Libya would likely be much better today under Gaddafi. Though the Iraq and Libyan wars imposed unintended consequences that drained our treasury, killed over 3,000 soldiers, and threatened the regional balance of power, our response to the SARS-CoV-2 (COVID 19) will pose unintended consequences epoch proportions for the next several years.

With poverty rates declining and average household income increasing (https://www.census.gov/topics/income-poverty/poverty.html), the Trump Administration was cruising toward easy reelection until SARS-CoV-2 arrived in the United States. Facing the worse respiratory virus since the Hong Kong flu of 1967, politicians, with public health experts' advice, felt compelled to do something to prevent the expected widespread carnage of the virus. Though the virus has caused over 300,000 deaths, the government's response to SARS-CoV-2 produces unintended consequences that will last long after the pandemic subsides.

SARS-Cov-2 is scaring everyone around the world. As it stands now, the fear of the virus alone will probably cause more destruction than the virus itself. Since our current generation of Americans has little experience with global pandemics of epoch proportions—such as the 1918 flu pandemic or the various outbreaks of the bubonic plague that devastated global populations before the discovery of antibiotics—many of us in the developed world lack the personal experience to measure the true ferocity of SARS-Cov-2.

The tiny SARS-Cov-2, based on antibody test results, might be as bad as or slightly worse than the deadlier strains of the seasonal influenza virus that kills thousands of people each year. The flu killed 80,000 people in the United States in

2018, a significant number but not as deadly as the 675,000 deaths that the flu caused in 1918.

Public health experts projected that last year's flu virus would be more virulent than the typical seasonal flu. Nevertheless, cooler heads seemed to prevail among our politicians, medical experts, and public health officials. No one dared to suggest that we should destroy our economy over the influenza virus as virulent as it might be. Then SARS-CoV-2 manifested, bumping influenza out of the headlines and out of our consciousness. We had a new bogyman to worry about, a bogyman that seems to be as frightening as all the known deadly pathogens combined.

As scary as SARS-CoV-2 might be, this is not our first brush with deadly microorganisms; and it will not be our last. One of the most lethal viruses in the world's history, smallpox killed 300 million people around the world in the 20th Century alone until the WHO declared the world smallpox-free in 1979, with roots dating back to the Egyptian pharaohs, killed anywhere from 20 to 30% of those infected, a mortality rate that is substantially higher than most pathogens that we have faced throughout our history.

Though intrepid public health leaders eradicated smallpox, an accomplishment worth celebrating, we cannot conquer all pathogens; we can only contain them. Cholera, a deadly bacterial infection, kills an estimated 95 thousand people (according to the CDC), and tuberculosis kills between one and two million people worldwide each year. Though we can use antibiotics to treat tuberculosis and cholera, we have not eliminated these deadly bacterial infections' threats.

Despite the Gates Foundation's best efforts, we will have to continue living with these horrible diseases in the future. If humans have faced deadlier pathogens in the past and continue to face more harmful pathogens in the present, then imposing strict lockdowns is not a pragmatic way to control a non-apocalyptic virus, such as SARS-CoV-2. Hence, public health officials should reserve lockdowns for pathogens that have higher mortality rates.

Unfortunately, fear is driving our politicians to make decisions without regard to the possible unintended consequences. Anxiety is capable of spreading around the world even faster than a virus. Globalization, global politics, air travel, the Internet, mass media, and our current political environment conspire to amplify our fear of SARS-CoV-2 beyond rational thought. This fear fosters an environment of scientific conformity—those scientists deviate from conventional opinion risk banishment to the scientific community's fringes.

If there were ever a time to listen to FDR's famous 1933 inaugural speech, now is the time. "The only thing we have to fear is fear itself." Unfortunately, the media largely ignored Roosevelt's brilliant speech, which Roosevelt elegantly delivered to calm fear during the depression.

During the age of 24-hour news, the Internet, and social media, news organizations can expand their audiences and amplify their message more efficiently than any other time during history; that is a problem! Media conglomerates know that fear sells. By producing fear-laden stories, both mainstream and fringe news organizations can generate more likes and shares on social media, elevating their profile and increasing their profits. Unlike false, misleading, and fear-driven news stories of the past, inaccurate, misleading, and fear-driven news stories today live indefinitely in cyberspace. Like viruses themselves, these news stories have an endless capacity to reverberate through social media echo chambers, generating, even more fear, anger, and outrage. Therefore, we should view SARS-CoV-2 news stories with a degree of healthy skepticism, knowing that the virus may not be as harmful as advertised.

Because of the Internet and social media, modern media has a tremendous ability to produce stories that cause mass fear and panic, which can make mass conformity. Humans will often coalesce around a unified response to gain a sense of control over the uncontrollable, even if that response is not pragmatic or reasonable. Doing something, after all, seems to be better than doing nothing.

The media's ability to amplify its message through the Internet—Facebook, YouTube, and Twitter—gives them the power to move political opinion and force quick action, even if that action is imprudent and impractical. Furthermore, the media's ability to generate fear makes underreacting a nonviable alternative for politicians in this crisis. Many politicians are unwilling to face endless media scrutiny and a voter backlash for being accused of underreacting.

By deciding to lock down their communities, politicians forced other politicians to make the same hasty decisions. With many of our well-known media figures and celebrity politicians advocating for a SARS-Cov-2 lockdown, those who were apprehensive about a lockdown had little choice but to conform or face scrutiny. Unfortunately, many of our politicians failed to consider the tradeoffs they were making.

There are two worlds in the SARS-CoV-2 pandemic: The first world consists of the wealthy (tech entrepreneurs, politicians, celebrities, and professional athletes) and those who have guaranteed incomes (government employees, members of the media, teachers, police officers, and healthcare workers). Those who live in the first world have guaranteed incomes and have the luxury of supporting strict lockdowns because the lockdowns are not imposing the same, immediate unintended consequences on them. The second world consists of service industry employees (hairdressers, massage therapists, personal trainers, bartenders, waiters/waitresses, hotel staff, and maids) and small business owners (restaurants, bars, hair salons, and gyms). Those who live in the second world do not have guaranteed incomes and do not have the luxury of supporting strict COVID lockdowns because the lockdowns impose severe unintended consequences on them. Unfortunately, COVID 19 is causing both of these worlds to collide.

The world that one inhabits is likely to shape one's psychological response to the SARS-CoV-2 lockdown. Many of our elites seem to be endorsing this lockdown because they are immune to the resulting consequences. It is often problematic for a nation to implement policies that affect some but not others.

During World War II, many of our elites fought next to those who represented all social classes. Actors Jimmy Stewart, Kirk Douglas, Clark Gable, Audrey Hepburn, Josephine Baker, and others served during WW2. Major League Baseball players Ted Williams, Yogi Berra, and others served as well. In WW2, our leaders made decisions that impacted everyone. Everyone, including our elites, felt compelled to share in the sacrifice. Unfortunately, we may not be experiencing the same sense of shared sacrifice during the SARS-Cov-2 pandemic. It seems like those who are making the decisions are exempt from the consequences, damaging the social contract that unites all Americans.

Though she probably meant no harm, Nancy Pelosi's decision to showcase a $24,000 freezer full of gourmet ice cream during the lockdown demonstrates how out of touch many of our elites are. Furthermore, in November, a customer caught Gavin Newsome dining without a mask at the French Laundry restaurant, an ultra-expensive fine dining restaurant in Yountville, California. Austin, Texas Mayor Steve Adler vacationed in Mexico after urging his constituents to stay home. Our leaders' hypocrisy is causing many Americans to question the legitimacy of damaging public health policies and lockdown. Governor Newsome and other leaders' bad judgment undermine the sense of shared sacrifice our leaders should be conveying during the COVID lockdowns, undermining their credibility during a painful time in America when everyone needs to have faith in our leaders.

According to Jonathan Haidt, a social psychologist, people who engage in emotional reasoning allow their emotions to guide their interpretation of reality (https://www.thecoddling.com/). Dichotomous thinking, a trait common among those who engage in emotional reasoning, results when people view the world in black and white terms; these black and white thinkers fail to see the nuances and the shades of grey in a world with few absolutes. Those who engage in dichotomous thinking fail to understand that people are typically not good or bad (except Hitler, Stalin, and the Kim dynasty of North Korea, and Pol Pot); most of our leaders are in the middle. Many problems often require a middle ground, common-sense approach, an approach that many people who support the lockdown fail to acknowledge.

The United States government's strategy for controlling this virus is equivalent to attempting to kill a bee with a shotgun in a room full of people. The intrepid shooter may believe that he is acting in the best interest of those threatened by the bee, but the collateral damage is unjustifiable.

As well-intentioned as our current approach might seem, we cannot deny the unintended consequences that the lockdowns are producing. It as if the trusted sages of public and social policy ignored the potential unintended consequences the lockdown might make. Our leaders have seemingly failed to consider the short-term and long-term impact the lockdown might have on the economy and the people's overall health. These COVID lockdowns will detrimentally impact the middle and working-class's financial well-being, causing a ripple effect throughout the entire economy for the next several years. Additionally, the lockdowns will have a deleterious impact on health and educational outcomes. The unintended consequences our political leaders should have considered before the locked are:

1. The economic hardships on vulnerable families: The loss of income will make it difficult for families to pay their bills and put food on the table, creating anxiety and depression, which will affect the overall health of those without steady incomes. This anxiety and depression will likely force many people to self-medicate with alcohol and other drugs. The economic hardship combined with alcohol and drug usage will likely increase domestic violence in vulnerable populations. Additionally, we can expect an increase in the so-called deaths of despair, deaths caused by loss of employment, and social/economic status. Unfortunately, many hapless and hopeless Americans will choose suicide over chronic financial hardship. Domestic violence will likely increase as well.

2. The reduction of tax revenues: The business climate in California was already inhospitable before COVID struck. High taxes and burdensome regulations in states—such as California and New York--will continue to chase large corporations into the arms of the low-tax states—such as Texas and Florida, further squeezing the middle class in these once-thriving states. California's 13.3% state income tax rate is the highest in the nation, which is more than 2% higher than the next highest state (Hawaii) (2020 State Individual Income Tax Rates and Brackets | Tax Foundation). California also has the nation's second-highest gas taxes (Gas Tax Rates by State | 2020 State Fuel Excise Taxes | Tax Foundation). California even has a real es-

tate document recording fee, adding an extra $75 to $225 to the price of purchasing a home (County recording fees on real estate documents going up to $75-$225 Jan. 1 - The San Diego Union-Tribune. California is extraordinarily expensive when we add the costs of hidden taxes and fees to the average tax burden. Hewlett Packard, Oracle, and Elon Musk, the CEO of Tesla, announced plans to move to Texas. Elon Musk sites the strict COVID lockdowns as a reason for moving. Ironically, Democratic Party leaders from California and New York argue that the government should play a more significant role in helping the working-class and poor; however, their policies make it difficult for the working class and the poor to thrive.

With businesses losing money and fewer people working, we will likely experience a sharp decrease in tax revenues at all levels: federal, state, and local. This reduction in tax revenues will force state and local governments to reduce spending. A lack of tax revenues will cause school districts to lay off teachers and other staff, diminishing education quality for children throughout the state and affecting those most vulnerable. Cities will likely have to lay off polices officers and other employees. Other government services and programs will likely suffer as well. In response, desperate state and local governments will increase taxes on goods and services (sales taxes), corporate taxes, property taxes (through ballot initiatives), and income taxes. These tax increases will strain struggling small businesses, further pushing them to the breaking point.

With private insurance and tax revenues declining, there will likely be less money flowing into the health care system, weakening the healthcare system when we are most vulnerable. This diminished capacity may inhibit our health care system's ability to respond to future SARS-Cov-2 spikes in cases and future pandemics. We need a strong economy to pay for health care!

3. The deaths from untreated medical conditions: We can expect a possible increase in heart disease, diabetes, stroke, and cancer deaths because patients are too afraid to interact with the healthcare system.

4. The adverse consequences on student learning: While many affluent children attend private schools and receive proper educational support, many poor children participate in distance learning, a less-than-ideal method of receiving instruction. The United Nations Educational, Scientific and Cultural Organization (UNESCO) reports a long list of adverse consequences resulting from school closures: interrupted learning, lack of access to nutrition, gaps in childcare, social isolation, and other detrimental effects (https://en.unesco.org/covid19/educationresponse/consequences). Moreover, according to studies, "F" grades have soared during distance learning, an unintended consequence of school closures. Closing the schools and forcing students into distance learning will negatively impact students long after the COVID 19 pandemic ends.

5. The systematic destruction of small businesses: The arbitrary nature of the COVID lockdowns has had an unfair and detrimental impact on small businesses, the backbone of any capitalist economy. Several news organizations reported in May that 100,000 businesses had closed forever. Yelp also reports that COVID is responsible for 60% of business closures (https://

> www.cnbc.com/2020/09/16/yelp-data-shows-60percent-of-business-closures-due-to-the-coronavirus-pandemic-are-now-permanent.html).

The COVID 19 lockdowns have severely weakened small businesses throughout the United States. Since the lockdowns have forced many small businesses to draw down on their cash reserves to make payroll and cover other expenses—such as taxes, utilities, and rent—we can expect even more small businesses to close during the next economic crisis. Moreover, future business owners who have been waiting on the sidelines for the perfect opportunity to create their businesses will be more reticent because of our current government's actions, essentially killing the entrepreneurial spirit that catalyzes economic growth prosperity.

Sober-minded economists must be wondering why anyone from the middle class would save money their entire life to open a restaurant, hair salon, tattoo parlor, gym, or any other small business if the government has the power to shutter it during a crisis. Not surprisingly, large corporations—such as Facebook, Google, Amazon, Wal Mart, Target, Lowes, and others—will emerge from the pandemic stronger. After all, these large corporations finance the campaigns of those who make the decisions.

5. **Implement a capacity-building approach to solve political, social, and economic problems:** Keiko, the killer whale made famous in the movie "Free Willie, won his freedom after several years in captivity. Since Keiko was only two at the time of his capture, he did not learn many of the skills necessary for survival in the wild; he did not learn how to be a whale. Dependent on his handlers for food and companionship, Keiko no longer had the skills necessary to catch his fish and socialize with

other orcas, causing his skills to survive in the wild to diminish. The relationship between Keiko and his handlers was solely paternalistic. Keiko performed crowd-pleasing tricks for fish, making Keiko utterly dependent on his handlers for his survival. Keiko lost his capacity for self-sufficiency.

In a desperate attempt to habituate Keiko for his release into the wild, Keiko's handlers embarked on a costly, complicated campaign to teach Keiko how to be a whale. In other words, Keiko's handlers attempted to break the paternalist bonds between the handlers and Keiko by building Keiko's capacity by teaching Keiko how to hunt and assimilate with a pod of Orcas. However, this Herculean effort ultimately failed, for Keiko's desire for free fish and human companionship over-powered his desire to live independently of humans; he died in Norwegian coastal waters in 2003.

We can learn valuable lessons from animals or mammals in captivity. Removing an animal from the wild can make it utterly dependent on humans for its survival; that animal may lose the capacity to take care of itself if it returns to the wild. For example, Yellowstone Park bears have become chiefly dependent on humans for food, causing the bears' hunting skills to diminish. We feel good when we feed the bears; however, in the end, we are causing more significant harm to the bears by making them dependent on humans for their survival.

In most cases, the charitable among us seek to improve the less fortunate' s lives for altruistic reasons. However, in other cases, government officials, political leaders, and reli-gious leaders seek to make their constituents dependent on them for nefarious reasons. Politicians know the easiest way to obtain votes is to make voters dependent on government charity.

Forty-two years ago, Jim Jones, the charismatic socialist cult leader, ordered over 900 followers to commit mass suicide by drinking cyanide-laced Flavorade (Guyana's version of Kool-Aid) in the jungles of Guyana. This cataclysmic end brought about by the orders of a mad, paternalistic cult leader demonstrates humankind's willingness to consign personal autonomy and self-reliance to a self-aggrandized religious leader in exchange for security.

Jim Jones built his utopian empire by employing various mind-control techniques from George Orwell's 1984. Jim Jones built his Peoples Temple congregation by appealing to downtrodden minorities through his communist gospels. Consequently, this god-like figure amassed great wealth, political power, and influence at the expense of his naïve flock, promising his followers a utopian paradise for their allegiance. Jones' fanatical followers exchanged their pension checks, social security checks, bank accounts, worldly possessions, and their sovereignty for Jim Jones' patronage. In the end, Jim Jones exercised absolute power and control over his flock, as evidenced by their eagerness to sacrifice their lives based on the command of a paternalistic madman.

Jim Jones' authoritarian deeds are not novel, however. History is replete with paternalistic leaders who enslaved their obedient followers with promises and patronage. Government institutions, ruthless dictators, slaveholders, and religious leaders and institutions use paternalism to render their patrons helpless and dependent. A helpless and dependent patron is a docile and obedient patron. Throughout our history, governments and various institutions use a variety of tactics to pacify their followers.

During the 16th Century, William Tyndale liberated the masses by translating the bible into English directly from Greek and Hebrew texts. One might think that Tyndale was doing the Catholic Church a service by translating the bible into the masses' language. The Catholic Church vociferously disagreed, however.   This new English translation eliminated an important spiritual intermediary of that time—the Catholic Church. Armed with the new English translation, Christians no longer needed to depend on priests for access to "the word of God." These biblically literate Christians were free to think for themselves.

Unfortunately, the Catholic Church and King Henry the 8th did not like having their authority challenged. The Catholic Church preferred to maintain its control over the masses by making the masses dependent on the Church to lead to spiritual salvation. As a result, English authorities rewarded Tyndale for his great act of liberating the masses. Tyndale was strangled to death and eventually burned at stake for breaking the paternalistic bond between the pre-reformation Catholic Church and the legions of catholic parishioners who could not read the classic Hebrew and Greek text. Like the Catholic Church, governments around the world employ strategies to make people dependent upon them.

Many people fear that a large, out-of-control government will inhibit personal growth and personal agency. Immigrants have sought America as a refuge from overly invasive and economically stifling governments—governments that tend to hinder personal growth and obstruct one's ability to become truly self-sufficient. The American Constitution provides freedom to immigrants, allowing immigrants to chart their life courses in their quest to pursue life, liberty, and happiness.

Our drive for self-sufficiency has given America its competitive edge, partially explaining why President Reagan's cowboy image resonated so well with the American electorate. Former President Barack Obama personifies personal agency, and he rose from humble means to become the forty-forth president of the United States, proving that anyone willing to work hard can rise to the top in the United States.

Despite our admiration for the rugged individual, America is arguably the most charitable nation in the world. Countless young Americans have died in the name of freedom and justice on other lands. Furthermore, American aid groups canvas the world to improve the plight of the poor. Thanks to President Kennedy's vision, eager, idealistic Peace Corps volunteers share their knowledge and ideas with impoverished people worldwide. Even the United States military provides humanitarian support. No other country had the necessary assets to provide the massive logistical support to Indonesia following the 2004 tsunami and to Haitians following a devastating earthquake. The United States Navy delivered food, water, and other life-saving necessities to the desperate survivors. American culture and constitutional values hardwire empathy and charity into the typical American's brain.

Many politicians and community leaders accommodate each party's extreme elements at the expense of pragmatism, resulting in the government's inability to solve problems in a manner that reflects the values of all constituents. However, the Republican Party's adherence to this approach has caused Democratic constituents to accuse Republicans of benign neglect. This extremist approach only alienates and marginalizes voters, causing our Republican leaders not to solve our nation's problems.

Conservatives can no longer ignore problems that animate large segments of our electorate. Republicans must adhere to a governing philosophy that develops capacity while providing people economic opportunity and freedom. There is a conservative alternative, however. Capacity building conservatism is a practical alternative to the traditional "bootstrap" conservatism, an approach based on rugged individualism and self-determination.

The capacity-building approach does not aimlessly expand government services and programs. The capacity-building model aims to reduce government services and programs, thus reducing dependency. Therefore, this model is consistent with the conservative philosophy of limited government. Capacity building leads to self-sufficiency, which is the same message that civil rights leaders, like Marcus Garvey, preached before Lyndon Johnson's Great Society movement.

Republican politicians at all levels of government must take ownership of problems that concern traditional Democratic Party constituents. Republicans can accomplish this task by using their power and stature to mobilize communities and resources to develop programs that promote personal agency and build capacity. Through this approach, Republicans provide the vision and leadership; community-based organizations mobilize resources and provide recipients the tools to become self-sufficient.

Capacity-building politicians seek to solve problems at the local level without expanding government or creating new, expensive government-run or government-financed programs. Instead, local, state, and federal politicians can play a role in solving local problems by using their leadership skills to mobilize community resources. This approach would put Republican politicians in touch with constituencies who have felt out of touch with Republican Party politics.

Capacity-building politicians can use their leadership skills to tap into social service providers' existing networks by forming collaboratives, encouraging social service program coordinators to share limited resources. Capacity-building politicians can launch grassroots causes that attract the support of local, national, and international celebrities. With celebrity faces representing their causes and media support, the capacity-building politicians can move their communities toward a consistent mindset with our founding fathers.

Because politicians need obscene money to secure election

victories, political candidates seek contributions from various well-connected constituents and special interest groups. This vetting process gives the winning candidate access to a vast network of resources within the community. Politicians can mobilize these same resources to solve community problems. Moreover, politicians can use the "bully pulpit" to inspire people to act. For example, many educators have known that parents play the most crucial role in a child's education for years. Educators know that there is a relationship between parental involvement and support and academic achievement. A capacity-building politician can address poor academic achievement by mobilizing educators, community leaders, parents, local businesses, religious institutions, and the media to address poor academic achievement. Instead of creating new government agencies and programs, politicians can facilitate collaborative networks to address parental involvement. Therefore, the politician plays the role of facilitator. When necessary, that politician directs limited resources toward that cause. This new governance system brings greater accountability to the system, for politicians are not merely bringing pork into their districts. They are taking ownership of problems that affect their constituencies, a valid form of representation. In the end, Republicans would be responsible for making sure the capacity-building message resonates with their diverse constituencies.

CHAPTER 4: A GOVERNING PLAN

1. **Make Capitalism Work Through the Expansion of Employee-Owned Co-ops**: Though the nation's morals have evolved significantly since 1776, America's complex history regarding race makes it difficult to reconcile America's past misdeeds. The harm that Americans caused to African Americans in the past continues to cause pain today. For example, the stress and constant activation of the stress response system (HPA axis or HPA activating system) may have epigenetically encoded certain medical conditions into African Americans' DNA, predisposing them to hypertension and other medical conditions, diminish the quality of life, and lower life expectancy. Making matters worse, many African Americans have never enjoyed the same quality of healthcare as whites, causing these epigenetically-induced conditions to worsen.

Because of Jim Crow, redlining, and other discriminatory practices, African Americans faced more incredible difficulty accumulating wealth and passing that wealth along to their heirs, placing their heirs at a competitive disadvantage to contemporary whites. This economic disadvantage impacted African Americans who lived and attended school, creating further disadvantages that contribute to disparate outcomes today.

Professor Ibram Kendi, professor of African Studies at Boston University, has identified how schools teach African American history. To his point, our schools are responsible for ensuring that our students learn about the deleterious effects of the trans-Atlantic slave trade, the history of slavery, and the history of Jim Crow laws and racial segregation in the United States. African American history is American history, and we must learn from our past to avoid making the same horrific mistakes in the future.

Because of America's historically racist practices, many activists often employ the "fruit of the poisonous tree" argument to discredit the American government, our republican form of government based on the Enlightenment values emanating from John Locke and other philosophers and capitalism.

Unfortunately, some activists blame capitalism for disparate economic outcomes between groups. According to the "fruit of the poisonous tree" argument, since America was deeply flawed at its inception, the whole system that our founding fathers created is also deeply flawed and must be destroyed. Those who apply the "fruit of the poisonous tree argument support radical change, such as replacing our capitalist system with democratic socialism or pure socialism.

Some of Americas' critics argue that America was founded in 1619, the year slaves first arrived in the United States. Though the primary propagator of this theory, Nikole Hannah-Jones, makes a tantalizing enough argument to win the Pulitzer Prize for her 1619 project, her claims are profoundly flawed and oversimplified, according to some of her critics, such as Professors Glenn Loury, John McWhorter, and several historians (The 1619 Project: A Critique – AIER).

The most obvious fact that supporters of the 1619 Project ignore is that slaves arrived in the United States before the Enlightenment. England brought slaves to the United States. England caused the slavery problem, not the founding fathers. Furthermore, our founding fathers would not make the problem disappear even after we declared independence from England. Political necessity trumped ending slavery.

When the United States declared independence from England, a chain of events would eventually draft the United States constitution. Therefore, it was the Enlightenment values that gave birth to the United States, not preserving slavery. The philosopher John Locke and economist Adam Smith were not alive when the first slaves arrived at the Jamestown colony, meaning they did not influence the early settlers' values. Fortunately, the Enlightenment shortly began after the first settlers arrived in the United States, launching an intellectual and philosophical movement that would profoundly inform America's founding fathers over a century later. The Enlightenment values of reason, science, individual autonomy, universal rights, self-determinism, and the rule of law inspired the Declaration of Independence and the United States Constitution.

In the United States, power is divided between the government and the private sector and between the federal government and the states; power is further divided between the executive, legislative and judicial branches of government; power is further divided between our flawed two-party system government. This imperfect system that our founding fathers created prevents the federal government and any of the three government branches from accumulating too much power. Disillusioned Americans who despise our republican government and capitalism try to discredit our government system by impugning the founding fathers and the circumstances surrounding our nation's founding, committing the fallacy of moral hindsight.

The fallacy of moral hindsight occurs when historians and critics judge past historical figures and events through modern-day moral standards. In some cases, it is not entirely fair to judge historical figures and events based on our times' moral standards; instead, it is fair to judge historical figures and events on their times' moral standards. For example, former President Obama opposed gay marriage as a senator; however, his views evolved as moral standards changed, and he later supported gay marriage as president. Therefore, it would not be entirely fair to judge that President Obama's views were consistent with the times.

One of the most famous transformations occurred in Alabama. George Wallace, the staunch segregationist who once said, "Segregation now, segregation tomorrow, and segregation forever was a product of his times. Fortunately, Governor Wallace's racial views evolved. The progressive version of Governor Wallace in the 1980s was also a more racially tolerant time. As times changed, George Wallace's opinions changed to reflect the times' morality, earning the support of many African Americans (https://www.biography.com/political-figure/george-wallace). Wallace's transformation demonstrates how politicians evolve from one era to the next.

Though the founding fathers marinated in Enlightenment philosophy, they still lived in an era when governments worldwide did not appreciate individual autonomy, self-determinism, and the rule of law. The Enlightenment had not completely taken hold around the world yet. For example, England, the pre-revolutionary war ruler of America, did not abolish slavery until 1834. Like other parts of the world, parts of America practiced slavery, a practice that tainted our founding fathers and, ultimately, America's founding.

In reality, the founding fathers knew they would never succeed in uniting the original thirteen colonies if they abolished slavery. Jefferson, Adams, and the other founding fathers understood that what we now call the Overton window would shift enough in the future to make slavery an unacceptable and immoral practice that would never survive the test of time.   Though the founding fathers could not abolish slavery in the original thirteen colonies, they planted rhetorical and philosophical seeds within the constitution that allowed future Americans to free the nation of the moral stains of slavery, allowing America to fulfill its promises as outlined in the constitution.

Our founding fathers' apparent hypocrisy relating to slavery does not impugn the vision they embraced, a vision that provided future President Abraham Lincoln the moral and legal authority to set the nation on the path toward abolishing slavery. Inspired by this moral and legal authority, Congress passed the 13th, 14th, and 15th amendments of the constitution after the Civil War. One hundred years later, Dr. Martin Luther King obtained his moral and legal authority from the constitution to abolish slavery; he essentially used the constitution against those who tried to justify Jim Crow laws as a states' right issue. In his famous "I Have a Dream Speech," Dr. King proclaimed, "When the architects of our republic wrote the magnificent words of the Constitution and the Declaration of Independence, they were signing a promissory note to which every American was to fall heir. This note was the promise that all men, yes, black men as well as white men, would be guaranteed the unalienable rights of life, liberty, and the pursuit of happiness." (https://www.naacp.org/i-have-a-dream-speech-full-march-on-washington/).

Historians might argue that the founding fathers were merely products of their era, and their views would have been substantially different if they lived in a different era, under different moral standards and a different political environment.

By employing the "fruit of the poisonous tree" argument, critics of the United States implicitly embrace neo-Marxism as a way to promote more significant equity through social justice. Radical leftists intentionally rely on social justice's ambiguity to tug at the heartstrings of those who support the term's ideas. To the naïve among us, social justice seems like a significant value consistent with Enlightenment philosophy. However, many social justice leaders hide their nefarious intent in these innocuous words, causing many well-meaning social justice supporters to embrace the implicit meaning while ignoring these words' nefarious intent. In many radical leftists' minds, social justice's explicit meaning is: creating an egalitarian society that produces equal outcomes, essentially transforming the United States into a utopian paradise.

The popular board game Monopoly teaches us that even under strict rules, wealth tends to concentrate in the hands of the few. Even though everyone starts the game with equal resources, strategy and luck influence the game's outcomes. The results of everything we do in life resemble a game of Monopoly. For example, baseball's egalitarian rules produce disparate outcomes between individual teams and players. Though all teams play by the same rules, some teams enjoy more remarkable success than others. The New York Yankees have won an astonishing twenty-seven World Series titles while the St. Louis Cardinals, the second most World Series wins, have won eleven. Shockingly, the Texas Rangers have not won a single World Series, representing a vast disparity between two teams that play under the same rules. In Major League Baseball, the elite ten percent of players make substantially more than the non-elite ninety percent. Players like the famous New York Yankee third baseman, Alex Rodriguez, sign massive nine-figure contracts while the less talented players sign mere six-figure contracts. Even the most social justice-oriented baseball fans would not argue that the twenty-fifth man should not earn as much as Alex Rodriguez. Acting works the same way. No reasonable person would argue that a mere movie extra should earn as much as Denzel Washington, one of Hollywood's most successful and most bankable actors. Those who rise to the highest in our competence hierarchies tend to accumulate most of the wealth. While this economic phenomenon may seem unjust to those who champion social justice causes, we all benefit when society rewards the most talented, most productive among us. Egalitarian societies ignore this reality, which is why egalitarian societies always fail regardless of the leaders' intentions or degree of magnanimity. After all, "the road to hell is paved with good intentions."

Radical leftist activists, such as Antifa and other enthusiastic Marxist supporters, often commit the "fallacy of the utopian ideal" when they argue that a strong central government can eliminate all vestiges of inequality through collective action, creating an egalitarian society that is free of disparities. Those who commit this fallacy believe that an infallible collectivist government should regulate and control resources' distribution, thus eliminating inequity within society. To accomplish this goal, revolutionaries would have to destroy capitalism. Utopians would have to concentrate power at the central government, implementing policies that diminish autonomy strip individuals of their rights.

In a utopian (collectivist) society, the government transfers power and wealth from the business and corporate class to the governing party elites, much like the power transfer in George Orwell's classic novel "Animal Farm." In "Animal Farm," a group of revolutionary-minded farm animals overthrows the farmer, creating a collectivist, totalitarian society of animals that is worse off than they were before the revolution.

In a utopian collectivist society, the government party elites accumulate the same wealth and privilege as the bourgeoisie, the capitalists, manufacturers, bankers, and other employers. Furthermore, in a collectivist society, the party elites become the consumers of wealth instead of producers of wealth, creating an unsustainable economic system destined for failure.

In a utopian, collectivist society, the party elites rationalize their greed by arguing that they are merely doing the peoples' work. Since they are doing the peoples' work, they deserve a few benefits that the ordinary people in collectivist societies do not receive. George Orwell sums up this phenomenon well in his book, "The Animal Farm": "Some animals are more equal than others."

The republican form of our government works symbiotically with capitalism. The founding fathers had the wisdom to know that in a purely democratic system, the majority would have the power to impose on the minority. Fifty-one percent of voters would have the power to raise taxes on the other forty-nine percent of voters, causing tyranny of the majority.

Admittedly, our system is imperfect, however. Like other systems, our republican/capitalist system produces political gridlock, inertia, and economic inequality. The late Prime Minister Winston Churchill famously said, "Capitalism is the worst economic system except for all the others." We can say the same thing about the American political system. Unfortunately, many disgruntled and disillusioned Americans believe that the American system is irredeemably flawed.

It is imprudent to compare the United States to a utopian society that has never existed in the past and will never exist in the future because humans are inherently flawed and easily corrupted. In a utopian society, a corrupt ruling class can use its government power for its enrichment. The American system, which our founding fathers built on Enlightenment values, is the best system the United States will ever have. Capitalism is a crucial economic philosophy of the American government system that promotes freedom and prosperity for the masses, inspiring immigrants from Nigeria, Afghanistan, China, Vietnam, Mexico, India, and other primarily developing countries worldwide to become part of the American dream.

We know from history that communism and socialism have failed in virtually every country that has implemented these failed systems. Capitalism has lifted more people out of poverty than any other economic system. Even though capitalism is proven successful, Marxists and neo-Marxists, especially in academia, promote a utopian vision that seeks to eliminate economic disparities between "the oppressors and the oppressed. These so-called utopian intellectuals support policies that redistribute wealth between the wealthy and the poor, believing they can create a more equitable and just society.

Bill Gates, the founder of Microsoft, is worth approximately $120 billion, making him one of the world's wealthiest individuals. Gates did not take a disproportionate share of cash from the mythical "money pile," leaving others with less or without; instead, Bill Gates created his wealth. In other words, he created wealth that did not exist before he found Microsoft. If Bill Gates had not created Microsoft, then Microsoft's wealth would never have been created, and society would be worse off. Thus, poor people are not poor because Bill Gates is wealthy. Poor people are poor for reasons that usually have little to do with rich people.

Gates created a product that millions of people worldwide value and use, making Microsoft an incredibly successful business enterprise that leverages the law of supply and demand to his favor and society's betterment. Since Gates created wealth that did not exist before the establishment of Microsoft, the world benefitted. Bill Gates has made many of his employees wealthy; he has made stockholders wealthy; and Microsoft software and products have made the world more productive, improving the quality of life for almost everyone worldwide. Microsoft products are affordable for almost everyone.

According to Dr. Thomas Sowell, "Humans were born in poverty." Those who understand history, politics, psychology, economics, and Thomas Sowell know that it is impossible to eliminate poverty.   Disparities exist between the rich and the poor even in the most strident socialist and communist countries. Communist dictators often amass vast wealth. According to several sources, Kim Jong Un, the North Korean communist dictator, is worth approximately five billion dollars. The daughter of Hugo Chavez was reportedly one of the wealthiest people in Venezuela. Soviet leaders enjoyed many perquisites that were far out of reach for the average Soviet system.   The problem with communism: In a capitalist system, the business class produces the wealth that it consumes; in a socialist/communist system, the elite ruling class consumes the wealth that the working class creates.

To maintain a stable society, the government needs to ensure equality of opportunity for its citizens. The government can ensure that its citizens enjoy equality of opportunity by protecting everyone's constitutional rights, defending the rule of law, providing quality education, and supporting programs that build individual and community capacity. By providing equal opportunity for everyone, the United States government can enhance most Americans' economic well-being, reducing race-based economic inequality.

In economics, there is a false dichotomy between capitalism and socialism. Fortunately, a system that allows workers to own the means of production can function within a capitalist system. This hybrid economic model would allow progressive financiers to establish investment banks specializing in financing employee-owned co-ops based on the free enterprise system.   These employee-owned co-ops would resemble publicly owned companies. However, employees would serve on the board of directors.

Workers would form a partnership or workers' collaborative to establish a business—such as a factory and a restaurant/restaurant chain. Workers' co-ops would pursue private loans from a co-op investment bank. Once established, this employee-owned co-op would distribute all profits to its employees based on job title and performance. These employee-owned co-ops would operate side-by-side with privately owned businesses, proving that capitalism allows for greater freedom by allowing socialist ideals to prevail in a market-free economy.

2. **Create an online directory that allows consumers to make conscience-driven decisions**: Before the information age, consumers had far less information to make conscience-driven decisions when purchasing goods and services. Information on how well a business treats its employees (pay, benefits, upward mobility) and its customers was not as readily available today.

Today, we can establish a website that allows consumers to decide how they spend their money. This website would provide consumers with information on employee pay and benefits, charitable contributions, environmental impact, and political activism. Consumers who support the $15 minimum wage would not insist on the federal government to increase the minimum wage. Instead, consumers would have the ability to research the online directory to make purchasing decisions based on how well a business compensates and treats its employees. Furthermore, consumers who believe that climate change poses an existential threat to our world would not have to insist on the federal government to establish strict environmental regulations. Instead, consumers would have the ability to research the online directory to make purchasing decisions based on how they impact the environment.

3. **Identify effective governmental policy through "federalism"**: When the founding fathers wrote the constitution, they envisioned a government system that divides power between the three government branches and between the federal government and the states. The founding fathers recognized the importance of creating constitutional safeguards that prevent large states—such as California, New York, and Texas—from imposing their will on the smaller, less populated states. Our forward-thinking founding fathers realized that values and interests would differ from state to state and region to region. The founding fathers also recognized that voters in New York should not impose their will on Georgia voters. The founding fathers designed a government system to prevent the majority's tyranny, a system that would allow the populace states to impose their will on the less-populace states.

Humans' drive to rule over and impose their will over others seems to be encoded in our DNA. The world incentivizes leaders. Political, business, and religious leaders in every social advance through the hierarchical structure achieve a higher status and accumulate substantial wealth during the process. This drive to lead other people manifests itself early in one's life. Those who serve in the student body government become political leaders later in life.

Ambitious politicians often start at the school board or city council level and work their way up to state and federal offices. Often, those who achieve tremendous success run for the United States Senate and eventually the presidency. These ambitious politicians try to impose programs they implemented locally at a national level, creating a one-size-fits-all approach that contradicts others' values.

The exact process plays itself out in other institutions. For example, some teachers spend a few years in the classroom before transitioning into administrator positions to advance through the district leadership hierarchy. Many ambitious teachers and administrators attempt to influence the education system throughout the promotion process by creating new reforms. They often try to implement district-wide, with hopes and plans toward implementing their reforms statewide or even nationwide. Unfortunately, reforms that work at one school site might not work on other school sites; reforms that work districtwide might not work statewide; and reforms that work statewide might not work nationwide. Demographic differences, social-economic status, values, and economic conditions are a few factors that can determine what works and what does not work, making a one-size-fits-all approach to education reform impractical for systemic implementation.

The COVID crisis teaches us that a one-size-fits-all approach to implementing government policies does not always work well. Many public health leaders and politicians advocated for national COVID guidelines. In theory, this may seem like a good idea. After all, countries throughout the world have implemented universal policies, such as mask-wearing and lockdowns. However, in a country as large and diverse as the United States, allowing the federal government to implement national policies is not practical. Population density and the number of high-risk individuals working within a particular geographic region are two factors that might influence COVID infection rates. In other words, a respiratory virus is going to affect a city, such as New York, differently than a small secluded town, such as Glasgow, Montana.

In December 2020, President Trump signed the $900 billion COVID relief bill into law. The pandemic relief package desperately needs relief to small businesses and unemployed workers; however, the government's top-down approach fails to consider the disparate economic impact the virus has had on the states. Nebraska, Vermont, and South Dakota have unemployment rates of 3.5% or below, while Hawaii, Nevada, and New Jersey have unemployment rates above 10% (Unemployment Rates for States (bls.gov). Instead of providing a $600 stimulus check to individuals in states with lower unemployment rates, the federal government should have directed its aid to states that need it the most. Politicians can ameliorate this problem by shrinking the federal government's size and power; instead, we should give states more extraordinary power, allowing states to address their unique needs during crises.

Our federalist system seems to produce chaos in times like this; however, this is not necessarily bad. Fifty states have the power to implement fifty different COVID response plans. With these various responses, we can expect different outcomes between states, which can be advantageous to our country in the future. If our goal is to perform better during the next pandemic, we should appreciate our federalist system. Our federalist system has created fifty COVID response laboratories, each capable of testing different strategies. When the COVID crisis ends, the United States will compare data from all fifty states to determine which COVID containment strategies worked. Perhaps we will better understand the impact of the COVID lockdowns, informing public health policy for future pandemics.

Since the constitution allows the states to serve as 'laboratories' for social and government policy, Americans should be skeptical of politicians who support the widespread, systematic implementation of any government policies or programs without allowing cities and states to test these policies or programs first systematically. For example, Congress should resist implementing a national health care reform program without allowing states to implement their programs first. By allowing states to design and implement their healthcare programs, other states can analyze the results and decide whether they want to implement similar programs. This "federalism" approach allows states to implement programs that reflect their people's economic realities, values, political interests, and needs.

4. **Make the criminal justice system accountable to the people:** Black Lives Matter supporters continue to protest injustices in the American criminal justice system. Even though police shootings have plummeted to approximately one thousand per year, police departments across the country need to implement strategies for improving how police officers interact with the community. Additionally, police departments need to implement innovative criminal justice policies that improve policing, lower crime rates, and lower recidivism rates.

Since police officers are public servants, the public has the right to hold police officers accountable for their actions. To make police departments accountable to the communities they serve, politicians, community leaders, activists, and celebrities need to collaborate with local law enforcement agencies. This collaborative relationship will build greater trust and promote unity between police officers and the people they serve. We can allow police officers to feel like they live on an island.

Unfortunately, police officers are members of one of the most misunderstood professions in the United States. The uninitiated assume that police officers receive extensive self-defense and firearms training during and after police academy training. In reality, many police officers do not receive the necessary training to manage stressful, deadly situations. We expect police officers to perform well under fire like Navy SEALS, but without the same training as Navy SEALS. The fact that most police officers never discharge their weapons in the line of duty should tell us everything we need to know about their ability to respond to life-threatening situations.

The key for police officers to respond better in life-threatening situations is to build their confidence to react appropriately during various situations. Since most police officers cannot hone their skills through real-world situations—such as situations that require police officers to discharge their firearms—police departments need to provide additional stress training where officers can respond to various life-threatening situations. Though many police departments have sophisticated equipment to teach Police officers how to shoot during high-stress situations, department leaders need to allocate more time for officers to train, allowing them to use bio-feedback strategies to control their stress response during stressful situations. Moreover, police officers need to spend more time practicing defensive tactics skills (based on martial arts principles), essentially hardwiring these skills into the officers' brains.

Academies should train police officers to practice visualization to prepare themselves for a variety of situations. When practicing visualization, police officers imagine how they would respond in various scenarios without physically being in those scenarios. The brain does not know the difference between thinking about something and doing something. Practicing visualization builds those stress response networks in the brain, preparing police officers to respond in the same real-life situations. In essence, we need to train police officers to think like athletes. Great quarterback, such as Patrick Mahomes from the Kansas City Chiefs, probably replay the same Super Bowl-winning passes in their heads thousands of times before they throw those passes in an actual Super Bowl.

Terrence Roberts, one of the Little Nine, once said in a workshop, "Our greatest possession in life is a storehouse of ignorance." When bad encounters occur between the police and civilians, public members often make certain assumptions based on ignorance without fully appreciating law enforcement's difficulties. One of the best ways to lift the veil on law enforcement is to create greater community involvement. Though police departments typically engage the community in various ways, too many community members do not understand law enforcement's nuances.

Celebrities and community leaders can use their trusted status to build bridges between their local law enforcement agencies and their communities. Police officers, celebrities, and community leaders can collaborate with police departments by participating in civilian review boards, ride-along programs, and training programs. This collaboration between celebrities and law enforcement can allow police officers and the people they serve to understand each other better. Police departments should be reaching out to Colin Kaepernick to encourage his involvement in their agencies.

Over the past several years, American businesses have shipped millions of manufacturing jobs to China, strengthening an adversary with the stated goal of becoming the world economic and military superpower. This transfer of jobs from the world's premier superpower to the world's emerging superpower enriches the global business elites and Wall Street; however, this transfer of jobs hurts the working class and middle class. While President Trump made efforts to bring many of these jobs back to the United States, the global economy's realities will prevent many of these low-skill manufacturing jobs from returning to a labor market that can afford to pay pre-globalism wages. However, the United States has a primarily untapped labor force capable of performing many of these lost manufacturing jobs at a competitive rate with countries with low labor costs. That mostly idle, non-productive labor force is residing in our nation's prisons. Tapping into this new labor force will also allow the United States to solidify its supply chains, allowing our country to be less dependent on China's goods during times of crisis. For example, at the beginning of the COVID crisis, our healthcare providers faced a dire shortage of personal protective equipment (PPE). Many healthcare providers purchase expensive PPE from China with limited options, the country where SARS-CoV-2 originated. Instead of relying on China, our prisoners should be producing PPE.

Many of our prison inmates lack employment skills and employment histories. Without employment skills and employment histories, many of the formerly incarcerated return to a life of crime. Our criminal justice system should expand prison industries by bringing many low-skill manufacturing jobs back to the United States. This new, innovative strategy would reduce recidivism.

The goal would be to convert many of our prisons into factories, where inmates can learn employability skills while building an employment history. Any profits that prisons might make would offset incarceration costs. These profits, however, would not go to prison officials; instead, prisons would use the profits to fund prison education programs, job training programs, mental health programs, and inmate salaries. The inmates would receive a competitive salary that does not inhibit the factory's ability to compete in a global marketplace. Prison factory officials would deposit the inmates' salaries into bank accounts. Inmates would draw salaries from these bank accounts when they are released. This new prison system would better prepare inmates for release, save costs, and improve the quality of life for the formerly incarcerated.

5. **Reimagine the education system:** The more things change, the more they stay the same, which applies to the American education system. Local, state and federal politicians enter office proclaiming that the education

system is broken and reformed. As a result, these ambitious politicians often promote widespread, systemic changes to overhaul what they proclaim is a broken system. To implement these systematic changes, these precocious politicians conspire with the "education industrial complex" to implement new standards and curriculum in a manner that ensures employment and profits for an army of education bureaucrats, consultants, textbook companies, banks, and testing companies.

To ambitious politicians, education reform is a path to glorious political victory, allowing them to proclaim that the problem is solved and to "punch their ticket" for higher office; to frustrated teachers, education reform is a path to constant professional development, forcing frustrated teachers to revamp her curriculum to reflect the latest trends. Unfortunately, from the whole language to the common core, nothing seems to work.

Common Core is not producing the intended benefits. According to the National Assessment of Educational Progress (NAEP) 2019 results, average reading scores for four[th] and eigh[th] graders have dropped, and average math scores have remained flat since 2017   (NAEP Reading: State Average Scores (nationsreportcard.gov). These unacceptable results remind Americans why politicians should not systematically implement new programs without sufficient data to determine whether these programs work.

All education stakeholders must decide what students need to know to be contributing members of a constitutional republic. Furthermore, we must determine the knowledge and skills that students need to possess to compete in an information economy during the age of globalism.

The American education system is coercive, reflecting the manufacturing era that demanded competent and obedient employees. Many students attend school because the law requires them to do so. Human nature tells us that people do not like to be told what to do; forcing students who do not want to attend school causes some students to rebel against their education. Many of our high school students are not interested in the hard-core academic subjects (Chemistry, Literature, and Calculus), yet the education system coerces them into taking classes that are seemingly irrelevant to their lives.

Many students who attend school do so because of the economic realities if they do not complete school. These students who fear for their future do not necessarily like school; they attend school because their parents, teachers, and counselors tell them that a college education is a path to success, a path to a higher income, and a path to the American dream. In other words, many of our students do not necessarily attend college for their passion for learning; they attend college to education signal. According to the education signaling theory, employers do not hire college graduates for the specialized knowledge that encompasses a college education; employers hire college graduates because of their ability to persevere and complete the rigors of a college degree, to delay gratification, and their academic abilities (ability to think critically; ability to read, write, and communicate). Elite universities—Harvard, Yale, and Stanford—do the screening for the top employers. A corporation that hires a Stanford graduate knows that its new employee represents the top echelon of candidates.

The current education model is outdated, a relic of the industrial revolution. The assembly-line approach to educating students does a poor job of meeting the educational needs of individual students. Our education system does a great job of encouraging students to aspire to attend four-year universities. However, four-year universities are not for everybody. Instead, high schools should teach students to select paths that consider their interests, life goals, aptitude, motivation, and life situations.

The four-year university track is most appropriate; the community college or vocational track is most appropriate for other students. Upon graduation, many students are not sufficiently prepared or motivated to attend college, and these students would probably benefit from serving in the military or going directly to work.

Our education system still reflects a pre-information age world, a world where sages with PhDs exchange knowledge for a hefty price, and university libraries serve as the Parthenon of knowledge. In reality, the Internet provides us with almost all the information in the world. We can learn math, science, social sciences, and other subjects by downloading books from Amazon.com; we can access scientific research through credible government and university websites; we can watch lectures from great intellectual minds on YouTube. The education system needs to reflect this reality. The COVID crisis teaches us that college students can learn from their bedrooms' comfort and do not necessarily need to attend expensive brick and mortar universities.

Instead of sending students to expensive universities to acquire knowledge of a subject that may not provide them a significant return on their investment, we should create a system that encourages young people to acquire knowledge through independent study and inquiry when possible. This system would allow students to conduct research using the copious resources on the Internet: Amazon.com, government websites; university websites; and YouTube. Students would take tests similar to, but more rigorous than, advanced placement exams to demonstrate proficiency. Students would earn certificates in writing, United States History, and political science. This new system would be more equitable, encouraging citizens to become independent, lifelong learners capable of creating education plans that consider their interests, needs, and economic backgrounds. For example, Coursera an online learning platform that provides free online courses from over two hundred universities. Many of our leading professors teach these courses (Coursera's Mission, Vision, and Commitment to Our Community | Coursera).

Online learning does not work well for all professions. Nobody would want a Coursera-trained physician to practice brain surgery on him; nobody would want to drive across a bridge designed by an engineer who received their sole training on YouTube. Students who want to become computer programmers, engineers, nurses, lawyers, and doctors would still attend a university, receiving practical hands-on experience. However, these students would only take classes they need to become proficient in their chosen occupation. These students would still have the option of completing their general educations classes through independent study.

For the past several years, financial institutions and the federal government have injected billions of dollars into the education system. This cash infusion incentivizes colleges to hire more administrators and add enticing amenities, such as elaborate recreation facilities, such as rock walls, swimming pools, and fitness centers. Turning colleges into amusement adds unnecessary costs to a college education. Unfortunately, college students are borrowing additional money through student loans to pay for these costs.

The federal government's role in financing college debt ignores a simple rule in economics: When the government subsidizes an industry, demand typically increases. According to Forbes, student loan debt in the United States is currently $1.6 trillion, creating a student loan bubble in the United States that will likely burst one day. The answer, however, is not providing a free college education for everyone or canceling student debt.

Providing free college education will not sufficiently address the student loan crisis. Providing a free college education to every interested student will increase demand and escalate costs. Furthermore, providing every student with a free college education will likely produce a moral hazard, making college students less responsible stewards of their education since they would not be paying for it. Furthermore, the current financing system does not incentivize colleges to contain costs if the federal government provides free tuition to everyone.

Then there is the equity issue. Since some colleges are more elite than others, the taxpayers would be providing an unfair advantage to those who attend expensive elite universities— such as the Ivey League schools (Brown, Harvard, Yale, and Stanford). In essence, the government would pay for one student's tuition to attend Sacramento State University while it pays another student to attend Harvard.

There are viable solutions to the student loan crisis, however. Purdue University implemented a new option for paying college tuition: the income sharing agreement (ISA). Under the ISA, students have ten years to pay off their student loans. The payment amount depends on their major, the amount of money they receive, and the amount of money they earn. In other words, Purdue's ISA program incentivizes students to choose majors that offer a higher return on investment; Purdue manages tuition costs while providing a high-quality education to each student. Colleges and universities across the country should consider Purdue's approach (Purdue invests in students' futures with new model of financing | PBS NewsHour).

6. **Change the debate from climate change to conservation and energy independence:** Few political topics are more divisive than climate change. To climate change

activists on the political left, global warming poses an existential threat to the planet's health; to the so-called climate change deniers on the right, global warming is a hoax. The debate does not have to be either/or, however.

Wedge issues are controversial, politically divisive issues that politicians raise to divide or alienate the political opposition. Politicians often use wedge issues to elicit emotional reactions from supporters and opponents of particular issues. Climate change, which used to be called global warming, is one of the most effective wedge issues Democrats in their campaign arsenal. Democrats use climate science to bludgeon their opponents, pushing them to the fringes of the climate science political debate.

There are parallels between the Democratic Party's response to the Covid crisis and climate change. Democrats, especially those on the far left, approach COVID policies (mask-wearing, lockdowns, social distancing) with the same zeal as religious fanatics.

The human brain is hardwired to form different belief systems, essential for understanding the world, becoming members of different groups, acquiring power, and moving up in the dominance hierarchy. People who do not believe in God will believe in something. Believing in something—such as God, political philosophy, or economic philosophy—provides people a sense of purpose and belonging that makes life meaningful and stimulating. A person's beliefs become part of their social identity. Once this process occurs, people tend to categorize: "I believe in climate change." "That person does not believe in climate change; he is a climate denier."

Membership in the "climate change is an existential threat group" creates a sense of fellowship and self-righteousness that can be intoxicating to its members. Since the climate crisis group has accumulated significant power in the past two decades, corporate executives, politicians, and scientists must find it difficult to resist peer pressure, inducing greater conformity, promoting groupthink among our leaders.

We associate with the in-group, which in climate change includes everyone who agrees with us. We then contrast ourselves with the outgroup: "We believe in science." "They are anti-science." This type of in-group/outgroup bias is prevalent in the climate change debate, which prevents the two sides from forming a consensus on how to address the issue to prevent or manage unintended consequences, consequences that drive up the cost of living the middle and working-class Americans.

The history of energy is simple: Energy technology has evolved from less energy-dense fuel sources, such as wood, to energy-dense sources such as nuclear energy. The advent of fossil fuels displaced the burning of wood, which is energy inefficient and produces higher amounts of Co2. If history is a great teacher, we should expect newer energy-dense technologies to emerge in the future. Capitalism loves cheap energy, and the free market system provides sufficient incentives for energy companies to develop cheaper, cleaner, and denser energy to sustain economies throughout the world for the next several decades.

Climate change does not have to be a wedge issue. Most Americans support conservation, preserving, protecting, and maintaining our natural resources. Most Americans also support energy independence, allowing the United States to remain free from Saudi Arabia, Russia, Venezuela, and others for oil. Thus, changing the debate from climate change or global warming to conservation/energy independence and sustainability can unite the two sides of the climate change debate.

Our use of fossil fuels has created substantial economic growth in the United States and other advanced economies.

The ability to provide cheap and reliable energy is the key to economic growth. Therefore, our politicians need to consider the unintended consequences associated with implementing climate policies. These unintended consequences include the following: increase in gas prices; increase in home prices and vehicle prices; increase in home energy prices and an increase in heat/cold-related deaths; increase reliance on foreign sources of energy, and increase in the regulatory burden that places American businesses at a disadvantage against foreign competition. As everyone might expect, middle-class, working-class, and low-income Americans will shoulder a more significant burden when climate policy forces prices to increase. For example, California pays the country's highest energy rates, placing a more significant burden on already-burdened lower-income Californians.

The United States must also implement a practical approach to addressing climate change. Though solar and wind energy are clean on the back-end (the energy-production end), these two green technologies are not clean on the front-end (the manufacturing end), meaning we produce significant amounts of carbon when extracting the materials to manufacture wind turbines, solar panels, and batteries. Michael Moore addresses this issue in his YouTube documentary "Planet of the Humans." Since wind and the sun are not always reliable, power companies often rely on coal-burning powerplants to provide backup electricity when the wind is not blowing and the sun is not shining.

Nuclear power is the most reliable form of clean energy. Unfortunately, nuclear power is associated with nuclear bombs, the most destructive weapons ever created. This negative association causes many climate change activists to be squeamish about nuclear power. The Three Mile Island accident in Pennsylvania (Three Mile Island accident | nuclear accident, Pennsylvania, United States [1979] | Britannica) and the Chernobyl nuclear disaster in Ukraine (from the former Soviet Union) made nuclear power out-of-favor (Chernobyl disaster | Causes & Facts | Britannica), an unfortunate reality considering how safe nuclear energy is.